T0079879

CHILLIES

Edible

Series Editor: Andrew F. Smith

EDIBLE is a revolutionary series of books dedicated to food and drink that explores the rich history of cuisine. Each book reveals the global history and culture of one type of food or beverage.

Already published

Chillies

A Global History

Heather Arndt Anderson

REAKTION BOOKS

Published by Reaktion Books Ltd
Unit 32, Waterside
44–48 Wharf Road
London N1 7UX, UK
www.reaktionbooks.co.uk

First published 2016, reprinted 2021

Printed and bound in India by Replika Press Pvt. Ltd

A catalogue record for this book is available from the British Library

ISBN 978 1 78023 635 3

Contents

Introduction

The Sun fell in love with an Earth Girl, told the Maya. He kidnapped her, and to keep her for himself, he trapped her in a tortoiseshell prison. The girl's protective father came at the Sun brandishing a blowgun, but the sneaky Sun had planned ahead, and had filled the father's blowgun with chilli pepper. When the girl's father drew in a deep breath to shoot the Sun, his lungs filled with chilli and he began to cough violently. The father died before the projectile hit the Sun, but once it did hit, it stung the Sun so that he dropped his bride. She fell back to Earth, collided with the ocean, and shattered like a mirror into millions of pieces. The fish in the ocean dutifully put the girl back together again, and then aligned themselves neatly into a seine to deliver her back to the Sun. The Sun, however, had been made so hot by the chilli-spiked dart that the fish couldn't get close enough to reach him. They were left with no choice but to abandon the girl in the sky to become the Moon, and the fish, still in a twinkling net, became the Milky Way.[1]

From an ancient galactic creation myth to a modern weapon of self-defence, there is perhaps no farther-reaching spice than chillies. However, the global history of the spicy nightshade is only a relatively recent one. Venerated by Mesoamericans for millennia, chillies did not feel the world's warm spotlight until five centuries ago, when Spaniards returned from American exploration with their bevy of solanaceous discoveries. Its cousins the potato and tomato would eventually go on to take centre stage, but all the while, the chilli was quietly implanting itself into the culinary traditions of the world, waiting for its moment to shine.

It would not have to wait long: three decades after it was introduced to Europe by the Spanish, paprika peppers (*Capsicum annuum*) were being grown by Turkic monks in the Buda region of Hungary. Paprika would eventually become so popular that by the 1820s, it had all but replaced pepper and ginger in Hungarian kitchens.[2] It was then that the 500-year-old dish goulash transformed into paprikash and became the national dish of Hungary. Before the sixteenth century was over, chillies had helped shape the culinary identities of innumerable world cuisines: Cajun, Jamaican, Ethiopian, Indian, Thai, Sichuan, Korean and many more.

Today chillies have regained their rightful place as a botanical superstar. Chilli-eating competitions showcase strength and machismo, and chillies have been used as a stimulating aphrodisiac for centuries. In 1912 the American pharmacist Wilbur Scoville gave his name to the measurement of pungency used to quantify chilli peppers' heat. More recently, biochemists have discovered that the active constituent behind the pepper's heat – capsaicin – shows promise as a treatment for neuropathic pain, prostate cancer and leukaemia. This little book cannot possibly discuss each of the hundreds of varieties of chillies – a list that is growing by the day – nor will it attempt to. It will instead examine how the spread of one odd little berry changed the way the world eats and the way we hurt and heal ourselves, and the ecstatic mania that ensued in the process.

I
Taxonomy and Ecology

The genus *Capsicum* is a complex of a couple of dozen species and cultivated taxa that have yielded more than 400 cultivars worldwide. *Capsicum* is but one member of the Solanaceae family, or the nightshade clan. Aptly, the name *Capsicum* is derived from the Greek κάπτω (*kapto*), meaning 'to bite'; in the case of chillies, the fruit bites back. The original Mexican term, *chile*, came from the Nahuatl (formerly Aztec) word *chilli* or *xilli*, and this is the common name still used in Latin America and many English-speaking countries. 'Capsicum' in common usage typically refers to sweet, or bell, peppers in New Zealand and Australia.

Christopher Columbus named chillies 'pepper' after the spicy taste of pepper (*Piper nigrum*), but the two plants are completely unrelated. Of the five domestic species of chillies – *C. annuum* (bell peppers, jalapeño, paprika), *C. frutescens* (cayenne), *C. baccatum* (cumari, ají), *C. chinense* (habanero and Scotch bonnet) and *C. pubescens* (rocoto) – *C. annuum* and *C. chinense* are by far the most cosmopolitan. However, despite the great economic and cultural significance of *C. annuum* both worldwide and in Mexico, very little is understood about the species' geographic origins and domestication history.

Capsicum is a rather fetching genus, comprised of upright, shrubby plants typically less than a metre tall. Its natural habitat ranges from the sultry swelter of the Yucatán rainforests to the parching sere of the Sonoran Desert. Its leaves are simple and entire, with an asymmetrical, ovate shape, arranged alternately along the stems; its roots vary from a shallow network of fibrous threads to a sturdy taproot. Like all members

Basket of colourful *Capsicum annuum* cultivars.

of the nightshade family, its flowers are sympetalous; that is, the petals are fused at the base like a wee, demure skirt that surrounds the flower's sexy bits. The pendent, white flowers while lonely afternoons away in self-pollination, but they certainly wouldn't kick a bee out of bed. Cross-pollination yields more seeds and bigger fruit, but more importantly it contributes to genetic heterogeneity. Furthermore, in some

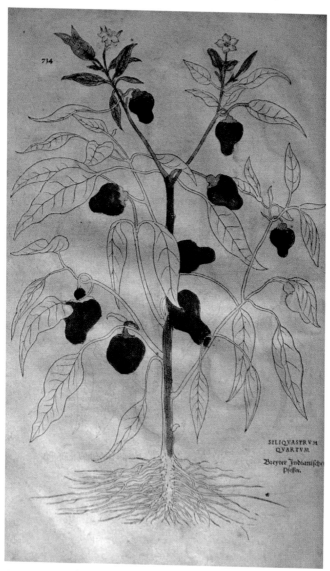

'Silaquastrum quartum', engraving from *De historia stirpium commentarii* (1542). This plant resembles *C. chinense*.

cultivars, the anthers (male parts) and stigmae (female parts) aren't mature at the same time, making self-pollination a rather tricky endeavour.

When that magic moment does occur, though: fireworks. The little white skirt, now a dry, dingy wreck, shrivels and falls away, revealing a berry developing in earnest, growing rounder or longer, yellower, redder or more purple, depending on the species and variety. Though it also includes the bell pepper, *C. annuum* typically grows into the classic long and skinny shape, predominantly sticking to shades of red and yellow, and similarly *C. frutescens* largely sticks to the elongated conical shape. *C. baccatum* comes in a variety of odd shapes like a bishop's crown or Brazilian starfish, and the brilliantly pungent *C. chinense* likewise brings us lantern-shaped fruits like the tam o' shanter of the Scotch bonnet and habanero. *C. pubescens* is the genus's odd plant out, not only producing leaves covered in fine hairs (hence the name), but purple flowers and black seeds.

Capsaicin

The chilli's fruit is more than just shiny vermilion skin or funny black seeds – it is also the manufactory of a cheerful little compound called capsaicin. 'The pungency of capsicum has been demonstrated to be due to a crystallizable compound, capsaicin, to which has been assigned the empirical formula $C_{18}H_{28}O_3N$', wrote the American botanist and pharmacist Albert Brown Lyons in 1920.[1] Produced by glands in the chilli's placental tissue (the spongy white part below the stem, to which the seeds are attached), capsaicin is but one of several capsaicinoids – potent, heat-producing secondary metabolites found in chillies. Secondary metabolites are

Habanero peppers at a farmer's market in Portland, Oregon.

produced by all plants to perform a variety of functions, most of which boil down to deterring herbivory. Plainly put, capsaicin is the chemical version of thorns, spines and stinging hairs. Because birds are unaffected by capsaicin, cayenne-laden suet cakes are much relished by flocking bushtits but avoided by greedy squirrels. More saliently, it explains why birds were the main distributors of chilli seeds for millennia before humans butted in.

As mentioned, there are six naturally occurring capsaicinoids, but capsaicin has the other five beaten in concentration and potency by a large margin, which is why the word 'capsaicin' is typically used in a broader sense to encompass all capsaicinoids.[2] The heat potency, or pungency, of peppers is measured in Scoville heat units, which are the number of drops of sugar-water solution required for dilution before the chilli's heat is no longer detectable (SHU). For example, as the baseline, the green bell pepper has 0 SHU. Jalapeños range from 2,500 to 8,000 SHU. The bhut jolokia, or ghost pepper, is strikingly hot with 800,000 SHU; pure capsaicin is 16 million SHU.

Professor Wilbur L. Scoville, pharmacologist, *c.* 1910.

As mentioned by Lyons, 'It is quite possible to form a reasonably exact judgment of the "strength" of [capsaicin] by the simple expedient of testing its pungency.'[3] The Scoville scale, used to measure chilli heat, was first developed in 1912 with Scoville's organoleptic test, which is conducted by mixing dried, powdered chilli in alcohol and then mixing the alcohol into a sugar solution, which is administered by mouth to tasters. The test is handy for measuring the ever-escalating game of chilli heat one-upmanship, but also had early applications in determining if capsicum had been used as an adulterant in ginger beer.[4] Unfortunately, because the test relies on human taste, it is frustratingly imprecise, and it is for this reason that high-performance liquid chromatography (a method of separating organic compounds for analysis) is typically used to measure pungency today.

The Scoville scale can also be used to measure other spicy chemicals, like piperine in black pepper and gingerol from ginger, as well as the world's most pungent substance, resiniferatoxin. Derived from the Moroccan resin spurge

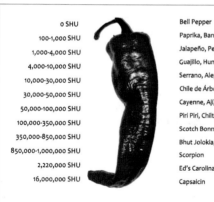

0 SHU	Bell Pepper
100–1,000 SHU	Paprika, Banana Pepper
1,000–4,000 SHU	Jalapeño, Peppadew, Poblano
4,000–10,000 SHU	Guajillo, Hungarian Wax
10,000–30,000 SHU	Serrano, Aleppo
30,000–50,000 SHU	Chile de Árbol, Manzano
50,000–100,000 SHU	Cayenne, Ají, Tabasco
100,000–350,000 SHU	Piri Piri, Chiltepin, Bird's-Eye, Habanero, Rocoto
350,000–850,000 SHU	Scotch Bonnet, Datil, Indian Tezpur
850,000–1,000,000 SHU	Bhut Jolokia, Ghost Pepper, Trinidad Moruga Scorpion
2,220,000 SHU	Ed's Carolina Reaper
16,000,000 SHU	Capsaicin

The Scoville scale.

Capsaicin molecule.

(*Euphorbia resinifera*), resiniferatoxin has a thousand times the potency of pure capsaicin – a startling 16 *billion* SHU.

Evolution

Capsaicinoid production, like that of all secondary compounds, comes at a cost to the plant. The trade-off between spiciness and seed-coat thickness can favour milder plants because plants with thicker seed coats are more apt to pass through the gut of seed-eaters unscathed. In wild populations *Capsicum* displays extensive variation in heat production; some individuals have exceptionally pungent fruits, while others of the same species may be milder. Since capsaicinoids are broadly antimicrobial and antifungal, in order to protect the all-important seeds from infection, there is an obvious evolutionary advantage to becoming very spicy. One might suppose that very hot chillies would also have deterred early human consumption, but it is likely that early humans selected chillies for use and domestication specifically because of these antimicrobial qualities.[5] In warmer climates, where meat spoilage has historically been a greater risk, there is concurrently a stronger cultural preference for spicier foods.

'Spices taste good because they are good for us', explain the Cornell neurobiology researchers Paul W. Sherman and Jennifer Billing.[6] In one study they examined more than

4,500 meat-based recipes from 93 different cookbooks, and found that spices somewhat 'cleansed' foods of pathogens.[7] Previously anthropologists had assumed that spices were used to mask the flavour of spoiled foods or to increase perspiration (certainly important in hotter climates), but the reasons humans uses spices are a bit more self-serving. A preference (or at least tolerance) for spicy foods may have literally meant the difference between life and death for societies susceptible to food poisoning. The human quest for a longer, healthier life led to a wider variety of chillies, in yet another example of plants and humans simultaneously driving one another's evolution.

A densely packed and intertwined stand of approximately 18 individual Chiltepin plants (*Capsicum annuum* var. *glabriusculum*), located in a garden in Austin, Texas.

Chiltepin

Wild chillies still exist in North America. The fruit from the upright shrub called chiltepin, chiltecpin or chilli tepin (*C. annuum* var. *glabriusculum*) is still gathered in Sonora and the mountain ranges of the deserts of southern Arizona from September until January. Entire families camp out in the hills during harvest season, collecting loads for selling and for personal use. With its name derived from the Nahuatl *tecpin*, or 'flea', this diminutive red berry is said to be *arrebatado*, meaning 'half-cocked' or in a hurry. In this case, the expression pertains to the tiny chilli's heat: intense, but dissipating quickly, like a furious little man coming out fisticuffs, only to exhaust himself immediately. The artist and botanist Jean Andrews recalled her south Texas childhood in which children using colourful language had their mouths washed out with chiltepin rather than soap, a punishment harkening back to pre-Columbian parenting techniques.[8]

The fruit from the chiltepin is a total roll of the dice; its heat is at the whims of a combination of heredity, climate and regional differences. Such genetic and phenological variation makes the chiltepin an exciting wild card for harvesters. During a drought year, when the plant's struggle for survival is more pronounced, the shrub won't waste its time on capsaicin production, and the chillies that year will be milder. During normal rainfall years, though, the little chilli is a firecracker, producing heat with abandon.

In the fifth millennium BCE pre-Columbian Americans began tinkering with the genomes of chillies at the same time that they were experimenting with maize.[9] Although it took early humans thousands of years to make chillies that were large and mild enough to be treated as a vegetable rather than solely as a spice, in recent centuries the chilli has been

Fresh chilaca peppers at a farmer's market in Portland, Oregon. When dried, chilacas are known as pasilla peppers.

crucial not just as an article of diet but to the culinary identity of Mesoamerica and South America. These foods formed principal elements of the cultures of early Mesoamerican civilizations, and continue to be staples of Mexican, Central and South American cuisine today.

2
American Roots

For early Americans, the Three Sisters – beans, maize (corn) and squash – were more or less the top items on the menu, but chillies were the cherry on top that no one would cook without. Archaeological evidence from throughout the New World suggests that the pre-Hispanic use of chillies was widespread; chilli residues and seeds have been found in rubbish pits, fire pits and ceramics, both in domestic sites and in treasure caches. Chillies spiked drinking chocolate and the maize gruel *atole*; they were offerings to dead elites, and ground into salsas to flavour foods for gods and chiefs.

Post-contact, the chilli became most important in the areas with the heaviest Spanish influence and control, largely because of chilli's commodity value as a tribute item for alpha males both local and foreign.[1] Chillies were a form of currency. The Spanish were greedy and spice-hungry in their own right, but seeing the great economic and cultural power chillies had in the New World certainly added to their value. An examination of fifteenth-century Spanish cookbooks reflects both the medieval European preference for heavily seasoned foods and the aesthetic influences of Ottoman cooks. Liberal use of expensive spices (especially pepper and ginger, both high in capsaicinoids) not only improved the shelf life of perishable foods but ably demonstrated one's wealth.

In the Americas the chilli's nutritive qualities were sufficient to keep locals interested, but it needed a significant boost before it could be catapulted into the international spotlight. It would take time before chillies transformed from harsh little berries towards anything resembling a civilized vegetable, but early Americans were certainly up to the task.

Pre-Columbian Domestication

Wild chillies are still harvested in Mexico and Central and South America today, though the vast majority of chillies are derived from five strains domesticated approximately seven or eight millennia ago.[2] The chiltepin is considered by molecular botanists to be the progenitor of the first cultivated chillies. The first domesticated chillies were the daughters of this plant – an anthropologic event that took at least five independent attempts over several centuries, from at least three separate genetic *Capsicum* lineages.[3]

The domestication occurred over several different instances and from a handful of separate species, evidence that the peppers, once tamed, spread so slowly to other areas of the New World that people in those other regions had already independently begun the process before other domesticated peppers had a chance to arrive. Similarly, other American crops spread so slowly that, for example, potatoes and squash each had to be domesticated several separate times. Due to a combination of factors, some American crops didn't travel quickly enough to prevent their reinvention somewhere else, a phenomenon that Jared Diamond attributes to the north–south axis of the Americas in his best-selling book *Guns, Germs and Steel*.[4]

If chiltepin is the mother of modern domestic chillies, central-eastern Mexico was their nursery, and the spicy fruits

Capſicum minimis ſiliquis.

Chiltepin type, 'Capsicum minimis siliquis', engraving from *Stirpium historiae pemptades sex, sive libri XXX* (1 5 8 3).

toddled off from there.[5] At first they were used predominantly for seasoning, rather than as a staple food, but archaeological evidence indicates that chillies were nonetheless one of the earliest domesticated crops in the Americas, dating back ten millennia. Analysis of groups of prehistoric starch molecules has shown that maize and peppers occurred together as a food complex and even pre-dated ceramics in some regions.[6]

Given the general absence of pre-Hispanic chillies in the archaeobotanical record, it seems that chillies may not have been widely cultivated in northwestern Mexico and the American Southwest until the Spanish brought them to the region. The anthropologists Paul Minnis and Michael Whalen suggest that in these regions, chillies were an item reserved for 'chief's fields'; that perhaps chillies were a prestige item rather than a staple food. In general, food was a powerful form of currency in the political economy of the area, but more tellingly, subfloor rubbish deposits at the Casas Grandes archaeological site in Chihuahua, Mexico, held not only charred chilli seeds, but crystals, copper, turquoise pendants and other kingly treasures that would have been out of reach for commoners.[7]

After generations of human intervention – selective breeding for fruit size, colour and pungency – three lineages and five taxa emerged. Of these, *C. annuum*, *C. frutescens* and *C. chinense* – known collectively as the *C. annuum* complex – originated from different forms of the same band of weedy chiltepin wildlings. The peppers that would become *C. annuum* came from Mexico; later, those that were eventually developed into *C. chinense* and *C. frutescens* came from northern South America.

The taxon that became *C. baccatum* (ají amarillo) was born of a wild species in Peru (*C. baccatum* var. *baccatum*), at the hands of industrious Inca horticulturists. It is still at the centre of *sarza criolla*, the Peruvian relish consisting of sliced red onion, ají amarillo peppers and coriander (cilantro). It is the pepper of choice for preparing ceviche.

C. pubescens, the *chinchi uchu* or rocoto pepper, is a purely domestic taxon believed to have no wild progenitor at all, having been domesticated from a weedy chilli to withstand the cooler temperatures of the Andes and the highlands of Costa Rica. (And it worked well. The rocoto is now a tender little fussbudget; even though most pubescent plants have the hairs to keep them shaded from intense sun, rocoto cannot abide the heat of the lowlands.) The rocoto is genetically similar to *ulupica* (*C. cardenasii*), a chilli species endemic to Bolivia and Peru that is purple-flowered and hairy like rocoto, but reaches only about half the rocoto's size.

Chillies drying in the sun in Cachi, Argentina, before being powdered.

Ají amarillo (*Capsicum baccatum*) peppers at a farmers' market in Portland, Oregon.

Myths and Legends

Because of their long association with chillies, the religions of early Americans often evolved mutually with their ethnobotany. To these people, chillies played a role in the birth and death of mankind. The Tupi people of the Amazon believe that after death, two giant worms consume the stomach and entrails of the soul (and the last remnants of earthly foods in the process), and then a god called Patobkia administers chilli juice to the spirit's eyes, restoring its sight and granting it entry into the afterlife.

Chillies were deified by western Pueblo peoples of the southwestern United States, the Hopi and the Zuni, as the fleet-footed Tsil kachina – a racer kachina (supernatural being) that embodies health, fertility and vigour. The Tsil kachina challenges village men to footraces. The men who lose are given a mouthful of spicy chillies, and the winner is rewarded with a scroll of fine piki bread made from sky-blue cornmeal.

The Inca revered chillies as the deity Ayar Uchu ('the peppery one'): the earth god of the West, son of the sun god Inti, brother to the first Inca and ancestor of all Inca people.[8] One day, according to Inca legend, all of the eight children of Inti emerged from a cave at a sacred place called Pacaritambo. They took up with some local folks called the Tambos and began the search for new fertile lands. The ancestors and their entourage stopped in a few places here and there, poking the soil with a golden bar to test its suitability for farming, sometimes staying long enough to conceive and raise children, until they came to a land called Haysquisrro. Here is where their journey took a strange twist.[9]

One of the brothers, Ayar Cachi, had a reputation for being something of a philistine and began slinging stones into mountains and cleaving them in twain, tearing the landscape apart and generally behaving boorishly. Fearing that Ayar Cachi was going to ruin the group's reputation, the others decided to ditch him. 'Oh, whoops, we've forgotten our tasty seeds and a bunch of treasures like gold and llama statues and such back in the cave', they said alluringly. Ayar Cachi refused to go at first, until his sister/wife Mama Huaco called him a lazy, good-for-nothing coward and shamed him into returning to the cave. After having fallen for the oldest trick in the book, he was then trapped in the cave by a large boulder that blocked his escape. The siblings and their entourage happily gave their brutish brother the slip and made their way to a stone hill called Huanacauri. As if on cue, a rainbow appeared at the end of the Cusco Valley. The soils were so loose and fertile that their divine golden bar sank right in.

From here, the legend's climax diverges somewhat; in one version of the story, the group ventures towards the rainbow and sees a stone *huaca* (shrine) shaped like a human, and Ayar Uchu is merged with it. When his siblings try to pry him loose, he tells them not to bother; that he is happy to sacrifice himself on the behalf of mankind, and wishes them well in all their endeavours. All he asks in return is for them to venerate him in ceremonies and make offerings to him – to just keep treating him like a deity, for old times' sake.

In another, more psychedelic, version of the story, our hero Ayar Uchu stands on Huanacauri, and as he opens his arms, they spread into great wings, with which he flies into the heavens. When he returns, he tells everyone he has been chatting with their dear old dad, the sun god Inti, who had asked Ayar Uchu to dictate a message. 'Tell them your brother Ayar Manco is the supreme boss now, and his new name is Manco Capac', Ayar Uchu relays, adding that Inti had said they should keep going until they reached Cusco. After having successfully delivered his divine instructions, Ayar Uchu is

Interior of the rocoto pepper (*Capsicum pubescens*).

turned into stone and becames an important worship site for the Inca.[10] This shrine served as the inspiration for Machu Picchu, the fifteenth-century cultural site, built as a miniature model of Huanacauri.[11]

Staff of Life

Chillies held a place of similarly high honour in the daily lives of early Mesoamericans. The Tz'utujil people of Guatemala (a Mayan ethnic group) say that when the vegetable spirits began to gripe to God about the way humans treated them, it was Tomato and Chilli that came to mankind's defence, assuring God that not all people were bad.

Chillies were a crucial source of iron when animal proteins weren't available. In early pictographs the Aztec people used the colour red to fill the speech scrolls (the Nahuatl version of a comic-book speech balloon) drawn in front of the image

Chilli *ristras* in Santa Fe, New Mexico.

Woman with *ristras* of dried chillies at her home in Concho, Arizona.

of a person's face. To denote that a person is speaking with intensity, notes the Aztec anthropologist Manuel Aguilar-Moreno, the Aztec added the word *chiltic*, meaning 'red'. It is because red is the colour of chillies that *chiltic* was so tightly connected with heated speech.

Chillies were so central to the diet of early Mexicans that they were as vital as salt for seasoning food; eating any meal without chillies constituted a fast.[12] On Columbus's second voyage to the New World, the journalist and physician Diego Álvarez Chanca noted that the native people ate a bread made of cassava and seasoned with chillies, 'which they also eat with fish, and such birds as they can catch'.[13] Álvarez Chanca had earlier noted that, besides gold and silver, 'there is also plenty of *aji*, which is their pepper, which is more valuable than pepper, and all the people eat nothing else, it being very wholesome.'[14] Álvarez Chanca was correct that chillies were very valuable; each province in Mexico was required to pay a tribute of 1,600 bales of chillies annually to Montezuma.[15]

According to the ethnographer Bernardino de Sahagún, one of the most important people in Aztec culture was the chilli seller. In his sixteenth-century account of Mexican daily life, known as the *General History of the Things of New Spain* (commonly called the *Florentine Codex*), Sahagún counts chillies among such treasures as colourful feathers, gold, semi-precious stones and even live jaguars and eagles as a few of the imperial tributes demanded in some cities. Sometimes these chillies were smoked, as chipotles are today. Smoking chillies dates back to at least the sixteenth century. Sahagún describes the use of chilli smoke both as a flavouring and a handy punishment for disobedient children. The Aztecs complained bitterly of unscrupulous chilli vendors who sold peppers from humid regions, where the chillies were too damp for smoking.

Post-contact, chilli use and cultivation among the denizens of the New World expanded greatly. Not only was there a wider variety of peppers for direct consumption, but indigenous people further north began increasingly to add

Chilli peppers drying in Isleta, New Mexico, 1940.

Arizona boy stringing chillies onto a *ristra* in 1940.

chillies to their diets. There is evidence that the people of the southwestern United States dabbled with chillies prior to Spanish contact, but the chilli would not begin to insinuate itself into the American diet until the sixteenth century.[16] Colonial-era Californians (still technically Mexicans) grew as many chillies as New Mexico and Texas. An economic boom in the late eighteenth century transformed New Spain from a subsistence culture into one that could afford luxury items, and suddenly the chiefly chilli was within the reach of average citizens. By some estimations, the average Hispanic family in eighteenth-century New Mexico ate hundreds of pounds of chillies every year.

Fabián García

Today, chillies are the quintessential New Mexican ingredient. The official state question of New Mexico (such a thing, in fact, exists) is: 'Red or green?' If one wants both, the secret handshake is 'Christmas'. Chillies can be added to any food, and even international fast-food chains like Subway and Pizza Hut offer roasted chillies as an additional topping in New Mexico. By far the most popular chilli in this region is the New Mexico Number 9, better known as the Hatch chilli. The development of the Hatch chilli began in the late nineteenth century by the horticulturist Fabián García. After much focused breeding, it was finally released in 1913. New Mexicans were overjoyed. 'To a native New Mexican', wrote Erna Fergusson in her *Mexican Cookbook*, '"chilli food" is something he keeps on wanting even in a new world of tightened geography and atomic bombs.'[17]

The Hatch chilli is ubiquitous in the Southwest. It enjoys an almost religious devotion from its fans – a fervour that sends New Mexicans from around the country back to their home state every September for bags of the freshly roasted peppers. People fill their freezers with Hatch chillies, terrified that they'll run out before winter is over. They buy vast quantities of dried chillies for stringing into the pendulous garlands called *ristras* and drape them about the house like crimson curtains.

Although the canned chillies available in most American supermarkets are typically roasted and diced green chillies of the same cultivar, in order to be called Hatch chillies they must be from the Hatch Valley, a scabby vale that hugs the Rio Grande in southern New Mexico. The high elevation and well-drained, fine-sandy Rio Grande fluvium – the Brazito soils – provide the unique terroir for growing Hatch chillies.

The flavour of a Hatch chilli is milder than a jalapeño, but hotter than the Anaheim, another of the New Mexico chilli cultivars. García notes in his 1921 article 'Improved Variety No. 9 of Native Chile' that, at the time, chillies were of inferior quality generally, and their thin skins and broad-shouldered

Fresh Hatch chillies from New Mexico draw a loyal following.

pods made peeling cumbersome (a matter of great importance to the chilli-preserving industry). Of most relevance to New Mexicans, however, was that Hatch chillies didn't pussyfoot around like some of the mild green varieties in development at the time. Garcia commented on his creation, with a certain amount of Zen satisfaction, that 'while No. 9 is not quite as hot or pungent as most of the unimproved varieties, it seems to be hot enough.'[18]

Mainstream American Adoption

As was the case with other New World foods like tomatoes and potatoes, the chilli pepper had to be filtered through the European culinary lens before becoming widely adopted by colonists in the northern reaches of America. Before García had begun his important work on developing

Roasting Hatch chillies over an open flame.

more commercially viable chilli varieties, 'red pepper' was appreciated more as a seasoning than an esculent. Cayenne pepper appears in several of Amelia Simmons's recipes; her *American Cookery* of 1796 – the first truly American cookbook – uses cayenne nearly as liberally as salt and pepper in these recipes. In her instructions on 'How to Dress a Turtle', she calls for equal parts of black and cayenne pepper along with nutmeg and mace (her instructions on 'To Dress a Calves Head in the Turtle Fashion' calls for a whole teaspoon of cayenne).[19]

By the middle of the nineteenth century, cayenne wasn't the only pepper on the American table. Fresh peppers were 'much esteemed by epicures', and early American cookbooks featured a variety of recipes for pickling and stewing them.[20] In the American West cowboys, rancheros and their wives

Spice canisters in a New York grocery store, with cayenne at the right. By 1900, cayenne pepper was an essential ingredient in the American kitchen.

brought ethnic Mexican cooking to the rest of nineteenth-century America with recipes for *chiles rellenos*. In Mexico *chiles rellenos* had long been part of a broader array of roasted chillies stuffed with various fillings, and covered in a range of coatings. There are more than thirty traditional variations on the theme. The standard version is a poblano pepper stuffed with ground meat and raisins, dipped in egg and then fried in lard to form a crispy, golden crust. The entire affair is bathed in warm salsa ranchero.

With its striking green, white and red presentation, another *relleno*, *chiles en Nogado* (chillies in white walnut sauce), is emblematic of Mexican national pride. It is said to have been created in 1821 for a banquet honouring Don Agustín de Iturbide, who signed the Treaty of Córdoba. The poblanos are prepared by being charred over a flame until the skins slide off easily. A surgical incision is made along one side and the seeds are removed. Then a picadillo, or hash, of shredded pork is mixed with almonds, raisins and other dried fruit, tomatoes, pears and peaches. The mixture is seasoned with salt and pepper, cinnamon, cloves, onions and garlic before being stuffed into the peppers. The peppers are blanketed in a white sauce of walnuts, milk and sour cream thickened with bread, and then pomegranate seeds and chopped parsley are sprinkled over the top. Ironically, the dish celebrating Mexico's independence from Spain is filled with almonds, sauced with walnuts and sprinkled with pomegranates – all foods introduced by Spaniards a few centuries prior.[21]

Chiles rellenos spawned a variety of American stuffed pepper recipes suited to a milder palate, as seen in home economist Maria Parloa's *Miss Parloa's New Cook Book* of 1880. These ranged from green bell peppers filled with rice and ground beef and baked in tomato sauce (or, later, canned tomato soup), to those filled with chopped ham and veal and

Chile relleno at Mi Mero Mole in Portland, Oregon.

topped with breadcrumbs. Modern *chiles rellenos* often rely solely on cheese as filling; one of the most popular progeny of this style of *relleno* has been the pub favourite jalapeño poppers. In this modern delicacy shredded Monterey Jack or cream cheese is stuffed into a jalapeño, which is breaded and fried until the pepper is tender and has achieved a napalm-molten core that instantly scarifies the palate tissue of the impatient eater.

Carne con chile, popularly known as chilli con carne – or stewed meat with chilli sauce – was another traditional dish that enjoyed adoption into the wider American patois. According to the culinary historian Jeffrey Pilcher, the Norteño interpretation of the dish ruffled the feathers of wealthy Mexican elites who visited Texas in the nineteenth century.[22] These aristocrats held a righteous disdain for the dilution of their cuisine and saw chilli con carne as a bastardization of their national culinary identity. If the chilli con carne had been served mixed with beans (or worse, on spaghetti, as it is in Cincinnati, Ohio), such indignation would certainly have been justified.

Cultural integrity aside, chilli con carne was invented by Latinos in Texas and began its ascent across the United States in the mid-nineteenth century, along with written accounts of 'The Wild West' and life on the frontier. In one telling of the Mexican–American War, *Chile Con Carne; or, The Camp and the Field* (1857), author S. Compton Smith describes it as 'a popular Mexican dish – literally red pepper and meat' sold by the Mexican rancheros that American soldiers had encountered near Monterey, California. By the 1880s Texas was peppered with 'Chili Queens' selling hot bowls of red from vast tanks bubbling away over a fire behind a table. These early American street vendors were folded into stereotypes of Mexican food and Latina women, which were both considered

Texas cowboy stirring a pot of chilli con carne in 1939.

San Antonio Chili Queens holding court over their chilli stand in 1933.

to be simultaneously alluring and risky. The parallels that
gringos drew between foreign women and exotic foods (as
being excessively stimulating and potentially harmful) were
nothing new. Fussy dieticians of the era, particularly moral
hygienists, had been cautioning the public for decades against
the dangers of both corporeal pleasures and heavy-handed
seasoning. The Chili Queens and their fare were, individually
and collectively, a breach of clean-living ideals and disobeyed
the tenets of so-called Christian physiology. This was perhaps
a great part of their appeal.

By the end of the nineteenth century, chilli parlours had
begun to pop up around Texas and Oklahoma as a sit-down
alternative to the ephemeral stands run by the Chili Queens.
These quickly spread to the Anglo-Americans in the Midwest
and beyond. Although they were more sanitized than the Chili
Queen stalls, and were, for all intents and purposes, the first
Mexican restaurants in the United States, chilli parlours were

still the antithesis of the dainty oyster parlours sweeping the nation at the same time. Chilli was still expressly for men – butch, manly men with constitutions brave enough to withstand the fiery chilli. But men could not contain the chilli's power for long. Chilli parlours were the chilli pepper's entrée into the broader American culinary landscape. Before the century was up, several Texas-based companies began manufacturing chilli powder (a combination of dried chillies, garlic and cumin) for national distribution, likely contributing to the successful spread of chilli parlours to the northern reaches of the United States.

The Americanized versions of chilli con carne that included beans, or called for the stew to be served on french fries, hot dogs or spaghetti, were a far cry from the purity and gustatory sanctity of meat and chilli peppers. Texans fervently maintain that the dish is their own creation, tending to forget the 'Mex' in Tex-Mex. But just as chillies allowed salsa to usurp ketchup as America's favourite condiment, chilli con carne remains a classic example of American fusion cuisine.

By the 1840s, it was the use of the word 'Spanish', not 'Mexican', in American recipes that indicated chillies might be a required ingredient, as in the case of 'Spanish rice'. But before it could claim the glory and fanfare for having exposed the world to *Capsicum*, Spain first had to wrest chillies from the American bosom.

Siliquastrum tertium, or Indian pepper, from a 16th-century engraving.

3
Worldwide Adoption

In 1493, after landing on the New World's shores for the second time, Christopher Columbus realized that the spicy foods of the native people were seasoned with a new ingredient, and enthusiastically reported his findings through his secretary Diego Álvarez Chanca, taking care to note that the chillies could net them a tidy fortune. In a cavalier manner, Columbus guessed that he could load about fifty caravels (a small, agile sailing ship) with peppers annually, which would bring in 200–250 tons a year.[1] Chanca, who was also the physician on Columbus's journey, was more interested in the medical uses for chillies. The men returned to Spain with chillies in the belly of their ship (and as it turned out, thousands of slaves, even though they had been specifically warned by their monarchs Ferdinand II and Isabella I to keep it civil with the natives). Thus began the Columbian Exchange, whereby hundreds of plants, animals, technologies and communicable diseases were transferred between the populations of the New World and those of the Old.

At first Columbus's crew seems to have overlooked chillies' potential as an esculent. For one thing, Native Americans ate an array of 'unclean' foods such as maguey grubs, tadpoles and tarantulas, and this greatly offended the Spaniards' delicate European sensibilities. At other times, trying new, appetizing-looking fruits had completely backfired; when the Spanish tried the lime-green fruit from the manchineel tree (*Hippomane mancinella*, affectionately dubbed the 'death apple'), Chanca reported, 'their faces swelled, growing so inflamed and painful that they almost went out of their minds.'[2]

Once chillies landed back on Old World soils, they were happily snapped up by green-fingered monks with a penchant for botanical oddities, and were grown for decades as ornamental garden plants. Europeans were still mostly wary of eating nightshades, though, and approached them with suspicion. However, unlike tomatoes or potatoes, which had only toxic counterparts in Europe, chillies looked different (they aren't *Solanum*, after all) and they had Old World analogues with black and long pepper, cubebs, prickly ash and grains of paradise. From the port-of-call at Lisbon, chillies sparked out of the Iberian Peninsula and crackled briskly through Europe via the Ottoman Empire. The chilli spread so quickly around the world that in Asia and Africa, everyone assumed it was a native ingredient.

Europe

By the end of the sixteenth century, chillies had made their way from 'Ginnie [Guinea], India, and those parts, into Spaine and Italy: from whence we have received seed for our English gardens', wrote the botanist and herbalist John Gerard in his indispensable *Herball, or Generall Historie of Plantes* (1597).[3] He lamented that due to a few chilly years (pardon the pun), the pods hadn't turned as red as he would have liked, but that he expected better 'when God shall send us a hot and temperate yeere'.[4] Fortunately for those dwelling in the Mediterranean climate, every year was temperate.

The Spanish *caballero* Gonzalo Fernández de Oviedo y Valdés noted in 1513 that in Spain and Italy, chillies were in regular use as a culinary ingredient. He also asserted that in addition to being a nutritious addition to the diet, they were better than 'good black pepper' for seasoning meats and fish.[5] Although chillies began to spread quickly to the south and east once they arrived on European soils, the Protestant Reformation may have been something of an impediment to the adoption of chillies in the cuisines of Northern Europe. It was Catholics who sailed the ships to the New World, and Northern Europeans were the first to protest the Catholic Church right around the same time. Consequently chillies were not much eaten north of the Alps until as late as the nineteenth century (mustard and horseradish, which also happen to grow easily in cooler climates, are still the preferred sources of pungency in those regions). As it made its way towards Africa, the Ottoman Empire was bringing chillies along for the ride across southern Europe, dropping peppers off in Germany, The Netherlands and England.

Chillies, predominantly in the form of powdered paprika, had centuries to spread out and get comfortable around commoners' kitchens. For peasants chillies were a slice of the good life. Unlike other spices, chillies weren't restricted to sultry jungles in exotic locations, putting them out of reach for regular folk; they could be grown in the average garden plot alongside chives and rosemary. Because of the attainability of chillies (and the fact that they were exceedingly hot), the upper classes largely treated chillies with a fair amount of derision. Reflecting this slow acceptance by the upper crust, the first European recipe containing paprika, according to the historian and chilli expert Dave DeWitt, didn't appear until the chef

Spanish paprika peppers drying in the sun for *pimentón dulce*.

F. G. Zenker's 1817 recipe for 'Chicken Fricassee in Indian Style', which appeared in the Viennese cookbook *Theoretical and Practical Compendium of Culinary Arts.*[6]

Unlike the Portuguese, who discovered chillies of their own accord in Brazil in 1500, Spaniards did eventually accept chillies into their diet, and even came to embrace them. The Portuguese brought the chilli to Goa, India, where it took off, but they didn't add chillies to their own cuisine then, nor do they use them much today. Although it seems to have travelled relatively slowly as an ingredient, paprika, or *pimentón*, as it is known in Spain, spread eastwards from Extremadura at the border of Portugal. Also hailing from Extremadura is smoked paprika, or *pimentón de la Vera*, one of the definitive spices of Spanish cuisine. Besides this earthy, smoked version, there are three types of paprika in Spain: *pimentón dulce* (mild), *pimentón agridulce* (moderately spicy) and *pimentón picante* (very spicy).

Like chilli-growing regions in other parts of the world, the town of Lodosa, Spain, grows its peppers on a floodplain (of the Ebro river). When the piquillo peppers are picked in the autumn, they are roasted over embers and then stuffed with salt cod that's been soaked until soft and then creamed with garlic and olive oil into a thick sauce that the French call *brandade*, meaning 'something that is pummelled'.[7] The dish, known as *pebrots de piquillo farcits amb brandada*, was likely inspired by the *chiles rellenos* encountered by the Spanish explorers, but with its *brandade* filling, the dish has been embraced by the French with as much enthusiasm. Recipes for the dish first appeared in Catalonia and Provence at the same time.

In the spring, when the green onions called *calçots* first emerge from warming soils, the people of Catalonia throw celebrations called *calçotada*. The onions are charred over open flame of burning grapevine wood, and after sliding the burnt exteriors off like a silk stocking, they are dipped in a luscious sauce of roasted red peppers and mild ñora chillies, called *romesco*. Thickened with ground almonds and bread, the sauce is somewhat reminiscent of the mole of the New World.

Peppers had been introduced to Italy from neighbouring Spain early on, but it was centuries before they were used with aplomb. The restaurateur Vincenzo Corrado called them a 'vulgar, rustic food' as recently as the late eighteenth century, but eventually Italy was won over on the humble esculent.

The chillies from Calabria, in the toe of southern Italy's stiletto boot, are as beloved by epicures as the piquillo, but for the opposite reason: they bring heat to everything they touch. Whereas roasted Calabrian chillies are a favourite pizza topping in Italy and abroad, in Calabria the chillies are traditionally used to make *'nduja*, a spreadable sausage paste flavoured with roasted chillies. The chilli is so appreciated in the south of Italy that every August the town of Diamante

Calabrian chillies from Italy are a favourite pizza topping.

holds the Festival del Peperoncino, or Pepper Festival, bringing upwards of 150,000 visitors. Festivalgoers laud their beloved peppers with chilli-eating competitions, growers' exhibitions and even a chilli-themed cabaret performed by clowns on stilts.

Also hailing from Calabria are peperoncini – the pickled banana peppers (*C. annuum*) used in salads, sandwiches and antipasti platters in Greece and Italy since the beginning of the twentieth century. Because of their bright acidity, saltiness and slightly spicy bite, pickled peppers like peperoncini and sport peppers are also ideal to serve on meat sandwiches, such the lamb-based Turkish skender kebap and the Chicago-style hot dog, respectively. Chicago also has its own style of the pickled vegetable medley called giardiniera, the primary difference being copious hot sport peppers in the Italian American version.

Although Italy's proximity to Spain made the spread of New World foods fairly easy there, most of the rest of Europe

Hungarian wax peppers (*C. annuum*) at a farmer's market in Portland, Oregon.

would need help from the Ottoman Empire to be exposed to the exciting new nightshades. After having successfully raided the Portuguese colony of Diu in India in 1538, the Ottomans could not contain their ebullience over discovering such a culinary treasure. From India, Ottoman Turks brought the chilli pepper everywhere they went, taking it to Bulgaria and then Hungary, where it would bask in the adoration of home cooks for centuries to come.

Shortly after the introduction of chillies in the second half of the sixteenth century, Hungarian tables were set with salt and paprika, not black pepper. It started out as a cheap alternative to prohibitively expensive pepper, making it an obvious hit with the peasantry, and from there it climbed the social ladder. When the trend-setting aristocrat Margit Széchy planted paprika in her garden in 1569, the spice began its slow ascent towards the kitchen.[8]

It took two centuries, but finally the landed gentry and the aristocracy began appreciating the spice, too, thanks to the ringing endorsement of Count Hoffmannsegg of Germany, who had tasted paprika while visiting Hungary. The upper echelons of Hungarian society began to learn to enjoy the unique flavour that paprika added to meats, sauces and stews. Hungarian gardeners now had a new incentive to begin developing new varieties of paprika in earnest, eventually creating myriad cultivars ranging in pungency from searing hot to cherry-sweet.

It was previously believed that Turks at Buda (now Budapest) had introduced the peppers to Hungary, but according to the Hungarian food expert George Lang, Bulgarians first began cultivating peppers in Hungary after being taught chilli cultivation by (and then fleeing from) the Turks.[9] It was those who had the most contact with Turkish invaders – the Hungarian herdsmen and servants – who most quickly embraced the fiery seasoning. *Paprikás*, *gulyás* and *pörkölt* went from being humble meat stews cooked in cauldrons over open fires to highly seasoned, hearty fare. Soon the brash new spice spread into the fish stews prepared by the fishermen of the Danube; *halászlé* is an anglers' paprikash, made with hunks of tender seafood swimming in a vermilion court bouillon seasoned with the tingly spice.

With their hot climates and rich, riverborne soils, before long the towns of Kalocsa and Szeged became epicentres of paprika production. Bolstered by the cheerleading of the prominent chef Georges-Auguste Escoffier in the late 1870s, France experienced its first (and perhaps the world's only) bout of Hungary fever, and *la cuisine à la hongroise* took hold of French restaurants.[10] Escoffier himself introduced chicken paprikash and goulash to his menu at the Grand Casino in Monte Carlo. It took a few centuries, but by the 1920s a plant breeder in Szeged had found one odd paprika plant that produced mercifully mild, fruity peppers instead of the typical pungent ones. Thus began Hungary's love affair with sweet paprika, which now dominates Hungarian chilli agriculture.[11]

Once breeders developed less pungent varieties, these could be dried, toasted, ground and blended. A range of eight grades emerged, ranked by qualities such as colour, fragrance and piquancy. Despite its timid fawn colour, *erős* or 'love' is the spiciest variety, as hot as the passions inflamed by the god that shares its name. *Különleges*, or 'special quality', is the sweetest, mildest and most carmine. The brick-red 'half-sweet' paprika (*féledes*) is a blend of several mild and pungent varieties, yielding a reasonable mid-range heat. The 'noble sweet' known as *édesnemes* is cadmium-red and just a mite hot; it's the most common Hungarian paprika sold in the UK and the U.S. There are also 'delicate', 'exquisite delicate', and 'pungent exquisite delicate' chillies (*csípősmentes csemege*, *csemegepaprika* and *csípős csemege, pikáns*, respectively), each with a rich pepper flavour and increasing piquancy; then there's the mild, fragrant 'rose' variety (*rózsa*), the colour of a salamander's belly.

Magyar herdsmen in Germany subsisted on paprikash as well, as noted by the German travel writer and historian Johann Georg Kohl in his 1843 account of Central Europe. 'Their principal nourishment consists of small pieces of beef, rubbed with onions and pepper and roasted', he explained, 'but the pepper – a Hungarian sort called "Paprika" – is used in enormous quantities. I swallowed a piece of the meat, and it felt as if I had eaten a burning coal.'[12] It wasn't just ethnic Hungarians sprinkling paprika across Europe like some wonderful paprika-fairy; other Eastern European countries within the former Ottoman Empire embraced warming chillies

The popularity of Hungarian *gulyás* surged in the 1870s when the pre-eminent French gastronome Georges-Auguste Escoffier introduced it to his Grand Hotel menu.

A variety of paprika pastes on display at the Great Market in Budapest, Hungary.

as well. In Ukraine (on the Hungarian border), Georgia and elsewhere in the Caucasus, thicker pepper pastes and dips are more common than powdered paprika. *Piros arany* and *erős pista* are made simply of crushed paprika peppers and salt, and are the two best-selling pepper pastes in Hungary. With hot peppers pulverized with coriander, cumin, dill and blue fenugreek, the spicy and complex *adjika* is one of a staggering variety of spicy red pepper relishes enjoyed throughout southern Europe with breads and grilled meats. In the Balkan region a milder red pepper relish called *ajvar* is eaten with every meal.

The Middle East and Africa

Throughout Europe (besides the Balkans), paprika and chilli powders were typically just a cheap and accessible substitute for pepper. However, the heat and sere climate of the eastern Mediterranean meant not only that chillies could be easily grown, but that their perspiration-inducing effects would be valued by the people living there. Perhaps most importantly, denizens of the hotter climates had already included a friendly nightshade as part of their diet for centuries before the launch of the Ottoman Empire. The aubergine (eggplant), another edible member of the Solanaceae, has several wildlings native to Africa and southern Asia, ranging in appearance from egg-shaped green or yellow orbs to red, pumpkin-shaped fruits resembling tomatoes (both the tomato and the aubergine are members of the same *Solanum* genus). The curious tomato-cousins were relished throughout Asia, Africa and the Arab world for centuries before Spain ever set its sights on new spice routes, and had been introduced to the Mediterranean by the early Middle Ages. This could explain why chillies were more readily accepted in the Ottoman Empire than in Northern Europe. Furthermore, and notably, the fruit of the Ethiopian aubergine (*Solanum aethiopicum*, also called the scarlet aubergine) is highly variable, with some members of the Gilo cultivar group bearing elongated red fruits with pointed ends.[13] To the novice, these are virtually indistinguishable from chillies and almost certainly set the stage for the chilli's debut in the Middle East and Africa.

With paprika (and the Ottoman Empire) as its emissary, the chilli pepper spread to the Levant and the Middle East, then to Maghreb and south through the African continent. Chillies were not transformative to Ottoman cuisine in the Middle East the way they were in Hungary, but they certainly complemented spices used in the pilafs, kefte (grilled meatballs) and roasted vegetables at the centre of the Middle Eastern diet. Ottomans set up market gardens in places they had conquered, allowing a steady stream of chilli peppers among other fresh produce.

Unlike in Europe, where chilli powders were more common, pastes of ground chillies and other spices mixed with olive oil were better suited to the culinary sensibilities of Middle Eastern cooks. While chilli powders were fine as a seasoning to be used sparingly, chilli pastes add a complex, fruity flavour component rather than simply piquancy. Some, such as Anatolian *biber salçası*, are straightforward purées made from sun-dried peppers and eaten with flatbreads or in pastries. Other condiments, like harissa, are more complex, blending roasted chillies with garlic and the carrot-family spices caraway, coriander and cumin (the Turkish spice blend called *baharat* covers much the same ground flavour-wise, but in powder form). Harissa is instrumental to Maghrebi cuisine, and pre-made harissa is primarily exported by Tunisia. In the Levant *zhug* is the harissa-like chilli paste that forms an integral flavour component of the Yemeni national dish, a meat stew called *saltah*.

Adding tart pomegranate molasses, crushed walnuts and breadcrumbs to the mix yielded a thicker chilli paste, similar to mole from the New World. The paste, called *muhammara* (*acuka* in Turkey), hails from Aleppo, Syria, which is well known for its peppers. Aleppo peppers, like the *urfa biber* of Turkey, are a moderately pungent, slightly raisin-flavoured *C. annuum* variety. Unlike the terracotta-coloured Aleppo, however, the *urfa biber* is black like a chilli negro or dried pasilla, but otherwise the two are fairly interchangeable in recipes.

The Aleppo pepper has been an unexpected casualty of the recent conflicts in Syria, which have effectively dried up Aleppo pepper supplies, shifting the plant's production and

Spicy, salty chilli paste known as *adjika* is used throughout the Baltic region.

export to Turkey. In maintaining perspective, it is important to acknowledge that the tragedy of losing 470,000 human lives far outweighs the loss of a single ingredient, but the Aleppo pepper is nonetheless a significant thread in the cultural tapestry of Syria. Some chilli importers have taken to unscrupulous methods to fill the shortfall, adding Korean chillies to the mix. With such a stark disparity in pungency between the two types of chilli, these substitutions typically fail to pull the wool over the eyes of buyers like the American spice retailer Tom Erd. 'Our business was founded by pirates', Erd lamented in an interview with *National Geographic* bloggers, 'and there are still some pirates in it'.[14]

It is because of Barbary corsairs that Columbus sought new trade routes to the Americas in the first place, but thanks to these pirates' business partnerships within the Ottoman Empire and North Africa, chillies easily found their way out of the Mediterranean, and south of the Middle East into Maghreb. The details surrounding the introduction of peppers into Africa are not well known; it may have occurred during the exchange of flora and fauna that brought slave ships from the New World to the slave coast of western Africa in the sixteenth century.[15] It was Guinea traders who likely brought peppers across the Sahara into North Africa, and from there they spread through the rest of the continent, both by the migration of people and with the help of Africa's keen-eyed birds. Birds were so handy at spreading the plants that chillies often arrived at the continent's interior long before foreign explorers did. For this reason, and the same reasons as elsewhere – that they are easy to grow, nutritious and cheaper than pepper – chillies became so integral to African cuisine that they are largely regarded by modern Africans as an indigenous ingredient.

A variety of dried *Capsicum annuum* (clockwise, from left): ancho, facing heaven, mulato, bird's eye and guajillo.

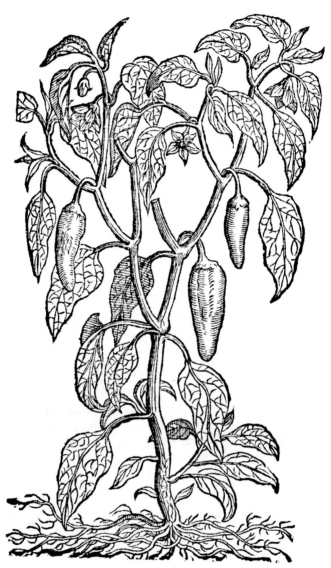

'Capsicum oblongioribus siliquis', engraving from *Stirpium historiae pemptades sex, sive libri XXX* (1583).

Portuguese colonists carried chillies to West Africa during their explorations, and brought their piri piri sauce along with them. The people of Mozambique were so enamoured of the fiery marinade that they use the name as a general reference to the tiny bird's-eye chillies and eventually adopted the sauce as their national dish. Namibians, Angolans and South Africans are similarly smitten by the slurry of puréed chillies, cayenne pepper, lemon juice, garlic and oil. After dropping chillies off in Africa, the Portuguese brought the chilli to African slaves working on sugar plantations in Bahia and Pernambuco in Brazil, culminating in the Afro-Bahian holy trinity of red palm oil (*dendê*), coconut milk and chilli. Outside of the American Southwest, Americans were slow to embrace chillies until they were reintroduced to them by the African slaves doing the cooking.

In Ethiopia the harissa-like paste called berbere is a complex mix of garlic, shallots and ginger, pounded with a combination of chilli powders and nearly a dozen spices: allspice, cardamom, nutmeg, cinnamon and cloves; maple-y fenugreek; coriander and cumin; black pepper and sprightly turmeric. The 3:1 ratio of chillies and other spices are mixed with oil or wine to form a dry paste used for slathering onto mutton or beef, or as the base of fragrant stews called *wat*.

In North Africa chillies surfaced in long-standing foods like merguez sausage, but curries and samosas are also quite common, illustrating a long connection to South Asian foodways, despite any lack of written records delineating it. The complex spice mix called *ras el hanout* resembles a chilli-spiked garam masala or a dry berbere, but regional variations can include endemic spices like chufa (yellow nutsedge seeds or tiger nuts, from which Spanish *horchata* is traditionally made); the black pepper relatives grains of paradise, cubebs and long pepper; or even rosebuds, saffron and galangal. Old recipes for *ras el hanout* often included poisonous belladonna berries or the ancient aphrodisiac known as Spanish fly (actually a blister beetle, *Lytta vesicatoria*).

In western Africa flavourful stews of meats, fish, vegetables and yams or cassava are emboldened by the addition of chilli powders. For the Yoruba people of West Africa, a feisty meat sauce called *obbeh* is eaten with mashed yams as a staple dish. The Dutch, English and South Asian influences on South African cooking bring a fusion of pungent sauces and relishes, garlicky sambals and a hot-sweet-tart apricot chutney called *blatjang*, eaten with the South African national dish – the meat-custard called bobotie. There are spicy, curried, oil-pickled vegetables called *atjar*, which, for the past half-century, most Afrikaans women have simply bought rather than make from scratch.[16]

It would take an entire book to properly illustrate the appreciation of chillies in African cuisine; each of the 55 countries on the African continent produces chillies commercially. Once they were introduced to the continent, the cooking of Africa became punctuated with searing heat. Today, only Asia comes close in its love of the chilli.

Asia

While Columbus was filling his ship with New World crops and slaves, the Portuguese explorer Vasco da Gama was on his own mission. If da Gama was ever going to lock down the spice trade, he had to beat Columbus to Asia. He successfully made it to India in 1498, and two years later another Portuguese explorer, Pedro Álvares Cabral, made his way to Brazil, claiming the rich, tropical wonderland for Manuel I. With direct routes to both India and Brazil, Portugal began doing many of the same favours for Europe (and damage to South America) that Columbus had done just a few years earlier; better yet, the Ottomans didn't much care about what the Portuguese were doing, and mostly left them to their own devices. The Spanish explorers had trouble from the Ottomans in the Mediterranean Sea, but the Portuguese were largely free to explore the Indian Ocean unmolested. Chillies, in part, drove da Gama's circumnavigation of the globe.

Lisbon had been a port of call for neighbouring Spain, and so Portuguese traders would have ample opportunity to sample the wares of Spanish ships that arrived from the New World before heading off to spicier pastures. The Portuguese made their own visit to Brazil only a few years after Spain, filling their ships up with chillies before heading off to corner the Asian spice trade. Soon, while chillies were clambering gastropodically across Europe through the greenhouses of botanists and enthusiastic monks, they were simultaneously flashing across Asia from India, east to Thailand and then to China, and finally Korea, with the speed of a brush fire, transforming the entire culinary identities of these countries forever.

Portuguese explorers, having little interest in chillies for their own use except as an antiscorbutic on long voyages, were setting their spice-trading sights on Africa, Arabia, India and Asia. Eventually Spain did make it to the Philippines, but it's not certain whether or not Filipinos had already sampled the spicy fruits during Muslim occupation of the area in the decades prior to the arrival of the Portuguese explorer Ferdinand Magellan. Unlike other exotic and rare spices, which were accessible only to the wealthiest classes, chillies grew lustily in tropical and subtropical climates and soon became the chief seasoning of the common people. Chillies became so firmly entrenched in the Asian diet that within just a few decades, even European explorers wondered whether or not the chilli was native to India or had been introduced from the New World.

After having been introduced to Asia by the Portuguese, chillies transmogrified curry and the entire cuisine of India. It is difficult to imagine the cuisine as anything but spicy, and yet, before the sixteenth century, pepper was the fiercest spice in the culinary arsenal of Indian cooks. Within thirty years of the arrival of Vasco da Gama, however, at least three different chilli varieties were growing in India.[17] The Portuguese explorers perpetuated Columbus's confusion about peppers, naming the chillies 'Pernambucco pepper' and 'Goan pepper'. South Indians, with their penchant for *actual* pepper (long and black, to be specific), relished the searing new ingredient. Chillies were easier to grow and store than pepper, and didn't take long to overtake it as the preferred supplier of pungency to vindaloo. Besides being hot and tasty, chillies were, in the words of Carnatic composer Purandara Dasa (1484–1564), the 'saviour of the poor'.[18]

By the middle of the sixteenth century, most of the chillies in Germany, England and The Netherlands came from India (via the Turks), and India is still the world's leading producer, exporter and consumer of chillies. Early on, most Europeans believed that chillies were indigenous to India, as demonstrated by the German botanist Leonhart Fuchs, who referred to the 'Calicut pepper' and 'Indian pepper' in his *De historia stirpium commentarii insignes* (Notable Commentaries on the History of Plants) of 1542. Of the forty or so regional cuisines of India, all but a small handful rely on the chilli to provide complexity to traditional dishes.

Chillies became so indispensable to South Indian cooking that in the city of Guntur, where pickles are a source of pride, chillies are even pickled in chilli oil. In Guntur they have their

'Capsicum latis siliquis', engraving from *Stirpium historiae pemptades sex, sive libri XXX* (1583). This form was later given the name *Capsicum chinense*, based on the assumption that it originated in China.

own varieties of chilli, the best known of which is the hot, thick-skinned Guntur sannam. Anyone who doesn't eat chilli is treated with side-eyed distrust. After the chilli had its coming-out party in India, meat stews and curries began to take on qualities of the layered pepperpots of Guyana, Trinidad and Tobago, marrying the culinary traditions of Native Americans, African slaves and South Asians. The casareep that distinguishes the flavour of pepperpots is derived from the juice of cassava roots, simmered down to a thick, bittersweet treacle and seasoned with salt, sugar, cinnamon, cloves and cayenne. The dish is not to be confused with Philadelphia pepperpot, which must certainly have come from African slaves; the primary differences are that in Philadelphia, tripe and ox heels were standard, the seasoning was brought by basil, marjoram and a cayenne pepper or two, and instead of dipping cassava bread into it, as they do in Guyana, the American version has egg dumplings cooked in the stew.

The curry stew known as vindaloo is based on the Portuguese stew *vinha d'alhos*, and as the name suggests, it calls for a goodly amount of wine and garlic. In Goa, the birthplace of vindaloo, a single pot of the eye-watering curry could include anywhere from ten to twenty whole chillies (split open to release the capsaicin-rich oils in the placenta), plus a dozen cloves of garlic, several tablespoons of hot chilli powder and a tablespoon of black peppercorns. In order for uneasy cooks in the British Raj to get it right, even vindaloo recipes intended for English kitchens were hot; the 1887 cookbook *Indian Cookery 'Local' for Young Housekeepers* called for what must have felt like a staggering half-dozen whole green chillies, seeds and all, split down the centre lengthwise.[19]

In 1511 the Portuguese made their first visit to the Siamese kingdom of Ayutthaya. The culinary intercourse between Thailand (as well as Myanmar, Vietnam, Laos and Cambodia),

Elizabeth Blackwell, *Guinea Pepper,* 1737, engraving.

India and China had been centuries in the making, with many of the curries, noodles and dumplings being shared across borders with small adjustments to reflect the preferences and resource availability of each region. Following their capture of Malacca in Malaysia, the Portuguese sent a diplomatic mission to the royal kingdom of Ayutthaya only one year after the establishment of their colony in Goa, India, and chillies could certainly have been a part of their friendly gesturing or gift-giving. Trade didn't officially begin between Portugal and Ayutthaya until five years later, but it is not known for sure whether India or Thailand was first to receive the great gift of chillies.

The game of culinary connect-the-dots, with Spain and Portugal as middlemen, explains the myriad, overarching similarities between Mexican and Thai cooking. Although Thai dishes would eventually make great use of other New World foods like pineapple, cashews, peanuts, tomatoes and culantro (a coriander cousin also known as long coriander), chillies would make the largest impact on Thai cuisine.

A variety of Thai chilli pastes available in an Asian grocery store.

Before long, Thailand boasted dozens of unique curries, varying by season and region, village by village. Massaman curry, or Muslim curry, was introduced by traders from Persia in the seventeenth century. The curry was so beloved by Thai royalty that its praises were sung in a romantic eighteenth-century boat song from Prince Itsarasunthon of Siam (later King Rama II) to Princess Bunrot: 'Massaman, a curry made by my beloved, is fragrant of cumin and strong spices / Any man who has swallowed the curry is bound to long for her.'[20] It must have worked, because she eventually married the prince.

Beginning in the seventeenth century, chillies found their way into nearly every Thai dish, especially condiments. *Nam prik*, or 'fluid chilli', refers to any of the hundreds of pungent sauces that can grace Thai tables, and usually consists of some variation on a slurry of chillies, shallot and garlic swimming in fish sauce, sugar and lime juice. These can range from simple seasoning vinegars called *prik namsom* and *prik dong* laced with sliced green chilli, to *nam prik phao*, sticky with sugar and sour tamarind. Some are more like a dry paste, such as *nam prik pla salat pon*, made from dried chillies pounded together with sugar, dried fish and shrimp, to be eaten with fresh cucumbers, lettuce and bitter gourd. *Nam prik maeng da* is flavoured with the flight muscles of the giant water bug, which purportedly tastes like some delectable combination of lobster, rose petals, orange peel, black liquorice and Gorgonzola cheese. When King Chulalongkorn, revered as Siam's greatest king, travelled through Europe in 1907, he wrote that it was *nam prik* and *khai chiew* (omelettes) for which he most pined.[21]

Eventually Thai gardeners would develop a few chilli varieties of their own, the most memorable of which is the bird's-eye (*prik kii nuu suan*) – the 'Scud' of the Thai kitchen according to Thai food scholar David Thompson.[22] Longer and more wrinkled, the dragon's eye chilli (*prik kii nuu sun yaew*) is milder; aromatic orange chilli (*prik luang*) is milder still, difficult to find outside Thailand.

In the 1930s a housewife from the seaside town of Si Racha, Thailand, began tinkering around in her kitchen.[23] The woman, Thanom Chakkapak, arrived at a sauce of chillies, garlic, vinegar and sugar, which she called *sriraja panich*. Chakkapak initially shared it with her family and friends to enjoy as a sort of cocktail sauce with seafood. With their goading, she finally went commercial with her sauce, and it was a smashing success. There are numerous brands of *sot siracha* – better known as sriracha – still produced in Thailand today, including Chakkapak's original (sold by Eastland Food under their Golden Mountain brand). Since 1980 the best-known brand outside Asia is Los Angeles-based Huy Fong Foods, but recently there has been a new wave of small-batch, artisanal sriracha sauces produced in the United States.

The chilli pepper may have travelled with the Portuguese out of Thailand from Singapore to Macau, where it would have gone to Hunan and passed through Guizhou on its way to Sichuan. Another scenario, posits Dave DeWitt, is that it came with Buddhists travelling from India on the Silk Road in the sixteenth century.[24] This makes sense, considering that the distance from India to Sichuan is about a thousand kilometres shorter than India's distance to Macau. Regardless of their path, chillies, or *lo chiao*, appear to have found a welcome home in southern China, holding high court in Hunan, Yunnan and Sichuan cuisine.

One of the most popular dishes from Sichuan, *gong bao ji ding* – better known as Kung Pao chicken – is a stir-fry of diced chicken, peanuts and dried chillies (celery is commonly added to Westernized versions), spiked with a generous helping of Sichuan peppercorns (another false peppercorn; actually the

Sriraja panich is reportedly the first sriracha sauce ever made.

fruits of the prickly ash tree). The dish was named for Ding Baozhen, the Qing-Dynasty governor of Sichuan, whose title was *Gongbao*, or 'palace guardian'.[25] Ding Baozhen purportedly adored the mouth-numbing dish so much that he brought it from his home in Guizhou. The dish was so closely tied to Ding Baozhen that during the Cultural Revolution of the 1960s the dish was renamed *hong bao ji ding*, or 'fast-fried chicken cubes'. The dish's association with the royalty of the past put it on the wrong side of the party line in the eyes of anti-imperialist Chairman Mao.[26]

Although the dish is popular with foreigners, many Chinese find Kung Pao chicken abhorrent for its use of chicken breast meat (often bland and dry in China) instead of cartilage, skin or the succulent meat found nearer to the bone, and young Chinese are often suspicious that the heavily seasoned sauce is used to mask meat of questionable quality. Kung Pao chicken is also, for many Chinese, a reminder of leaner times, since it was a dish that gained ubiquity after intense economic reforms. Nevertheless, the dish is loved by Westerners for its rich, tangy sauce and the bold heat delivered by the particular Sichuan chillies called *chao tian jiao*, or 'facing heaven' chillies.

Sichuan is home to numerous other spicy dishes: *ma po tofu* is soft tofu and ground pork sauced with black-bean chilli paste and strewn with crushed Sichuan peppercorn; the hangover-helper *dan dan* noodles consist of spaghetti-style wheat noodles in a fiery broth; and the cold dish of steamed poultry in sweet and sour chilli oil – 'saliva' chicken – gets its name from the condition it invokes rather than an ingredient. One of China's hottest dishes, however, hails from Hunan. *Gan guo*, or 'dry pot', is akin to a hotpot of chillies with meat, seafood or tofu, but without the bubbling broth to dilute the heat. Hunan cuisine tends to be less oily than that of

Sichuan, but the heavy-handed application of chillies results in blistering dishes like Hunan spicy beef.

The Chongqing-style hotpot is a pyroclastic meat broth seasoned with ginger, garlic and black pepper, made fragrant with Shaoxing wine; cinnamon; black and green cardamom; anetholic star anise, fennel seed and liquorice bark. This broth is fortified with a handful of dried chillies and Sichuan peppercorns, suspended in a mouth-coating slick of chilli oil, creating the *ma la* ('numb-spicy') taste. Often the pot is split into two sections (*yuanyang*), with one side containing a milder, medicinal broth, milky-white with pork marrow and chicken fat, seasoned with shiitake mushrooms, spring onions (scallions), red dates and goji berries. At its core, hotpot is a simmering meat stew cooked over an open flame, which makes it logical that the hotpot originated with the Mongolian nomads, just as *gulyás* came from Hungarian herdsmen cooking afield. After the Battle of Shanhai Pass in 1644, the newly

Traditional Kung Pao chicken made with 'facing heaven' chillies and Sichuan peppercorns.

formed Qing Dynasty would have been exultant to add Manchu hotpot to its culinary repertoire.

A number of chilli oils, sauces and chilli-bean pastes have flourished throughout China, with hundreds of commercially produced sauces available worldwide. Today China is second to India in production of dried chillies, but is the world's leading producer of fresh chillies, even growing the majority of those eaten in Mexico. Chillies are just one of the culinary contributions that China made to Japan, particularly with the chilli oil called *rāyu*.

Portugal made its first contact with Japan in 1543, and before the century was up, trade had begun in earnest. When Portugal introduced potatoes, tempura and refined sugar to Japan (resulting in the invention of *nanban-gashi*, or the delightfully named 'southern barbarian confection'), they very likely threw in chillies while they were at it.[27] Within a century, spice dealers in Edo (modern-day Tokyo) had developed a spice blend called *shichimi tōgarashi* (seven-flavour chilli pepper). The aromatic blend is a combination of cayenne, dried yuzu citrus peel, nori seaweed, white and black sesame seeds (or sometimes hemp seed), *sanshō* (Japanese pepper; technically another prickly ash, like Sichuan peppercorn) and ground ginger. *Tōgarashi* is a tabletop staple in Japan, perfect for shaking onto hot, brothy soba or ramen, or the sweet-savoury simmered beef and onion rice bowl *gyūdon*, popular since the Meiji restoration period of the late nineteenth century.

Acharazuke, or turnips with daikon, persimmon or lotus root, pickled in rice vinegar, sugar, salt (or soy sauce) and sliced red chillies, may have come from the Portuguese as well, who learned to make their *achar* from the Persians. Alternatively the dish could have been derived from the Malaysian pickle *acar* encountered by the Japanese in the early seventeenth century.[28] The addition of peppers came to Malaysia via India (who received them from the Portuguese), however, and the Hindustani *acár* and Urdu *ačār* both come from the Persian word *āčār*, meaning 'pickle'.

A Japanese chilli species originally thought to be the only one native to Asia was given the name *Capsicum anomalum* when it was discovered. In 1995 genetic data confirmed that it is not a chilli at all, and rightfully belongs in its own genus – *Tubocapsicum*.[29] First described in 1879 by the French botanists Adrien René Franchet and Paul Amédée Ludovic Savatier, the plant resembles the wild chiltepin of Mexico. Regardless of its place on the *Capsicum* family tree, the 'chilli' yielded by *Tubocapsicum* is but a sad, bitter little berry, and cannot hold a candle to the glorious *shishito*, *fushimi* and *manganji* peppers grown in Japan. Although the sweetness of these varieties reflects the Japanese preference for milder, cleaner flavours innate in a people raised on seafood rather than fatty meats, Japan's neighbours to the west would find hot chillies irresistible.

When Japan invaded Korea at the end of the sixteenth century, they brought chillies aboard their argosy as something of a culinary consolation prize. Although the Korean military official Yi Sugwang was not a fan, writing in 1614 that chilli peppers were a 'great poison', he did offer that they were popular in saloons.[30] As was the case with Indian and Thai food, Koreans would not know just what they had been lacking until they no longer lacked it. In Korea chillies would find a warm welcome.

Asia's first lactofermented vegetables date back to around 50 BCE in China, and the method was eagerly adopted by Koreans as a way to both preserve vegetables through winter and improve their flavour and nutrition. For centuries, kimchi was flavoured primarily with ginger, garlic, Sichuan peppercorns

Shishito peppers are one of the few chillies cultivated in Japan.

and tangerine peel (plus seafood, broth or meat), and these ingredients remained after the introduction of chillies to the pickles. By 1715 chillies had made their first appearance in written kimchi recipes, and a century later the majority of the hundred or so varieties of kimchi used red chilli peppers.[31] Koreans considered the colour red a good-luck charm, fending off sinister ghosts and otherworldly ne'er-do-wells. True to Yi Sugwang's words, kimchi is an excellent *anju* (drinking food), especially served sautéed with pork and tofu as *dubu kimchi*. A staple home-style dish, laden with vegetables and bits of seafood or beef, *kimchi jjigae* (kimchi stew) derives its heat from both kimchi and chilli powder, and is how generations of Korean mothers have used up kimchi that has gone a bit too sour for eating alone as a side-dish.

Another Korean staple, *gochujang*, is one food that, prior to the introduction of the chilli, simply couldn't have existed. According to the *Jeungbo Sallim Gyeongje*, a Korean farming and cooking guidebook written by Yu Jung-rim in 1766, fermented soybean paste was mixed with chilli powder and glutinous rice powder, packed into stone crocks and aged in the sun on a special part of one's property called the *jangdokdae* (soy jar terrace; modern Koreans often keep their crocks on apartment balconies).[32] The condiment somewhat resembles a very thick, spicy ketchup, and is similar to Japanese miso, but its sticky sweetness and heat make it better adapted to the Korean palate.

Along with *doenjang* (a miso-like paste) and *ganjang* (soy sauce), *gochujang* is one of Korea's three mother sauces; mixing it with *doenjang* and sesame oil makes the more complex

Kimchi, such as these examples made with daikon and Chinese leaf, was forever changed by the introduction of chillies to Korea.

Kimchi jjigae is how Korean cooks use up kimchi that's too ripe to eat fresh.

ssamjang, nutritious enough to be eaten simply with rice and lettuce as a simple meal. *Gochujang* is traditionally eaten on *hoedeopbap* or *bibimbap* (rice bowls topped with vegetables and either sliced raw fish or grilled beef and a raw egg, respectively) or used as a marinade for *bulgogi* (thinly sliced meats). It is the basis of traditional soups like the custardy tofu-vegetable stew *sundubu jjigae*, cardinal-red and served bubbling-hot in a stone bowl, and *boshintang* ('invigorating soup'), a 150-year-old recipe consisting of green onions, dandelion and perilla leaves, fresh liquorice-minty hyssop and dog meat.

Although Mexican-style salsas and hot sauces are still popular in the Americas, today, Asian hot sauces like sriracha are more popular worldwide than any application dreamed up by their progenitors. Chicken tikka masala, declared to be 'a true British national dish' in 2001, couldn't exist without the chilli (or the British love of gravy).[33] Spain may get the credit for introducing chillies to Europe, but the world has Portugal to thank for getting chillies into the right hands.

4
Healing Properties

In order to purify the body and mind prior to their psychedelic spirit-quests, it was necessary for Amazonian men to stick to a prescriptive diet omitting sex, chilli, salt and lard; after that, they were deemed worthy of drinking the sacred brew called *ayahuasca*, which would reveal to them the secrets of the universe.[1]

Most Meso- and South Americans, however, found chillies to be good medicine on their own, and the chilli was an important amulet in early American folk medicine. Once adopted by Western doctors, the sky was the limit for red peppers. Botanists and physicians from the seventeenth century onwards lauded them for their potency against forgetfulness, and by the nineteenth century they were celebrated as effective treatments against an array of ailments, including atonic gout, dyspepsia accompanied by flatulence, hemorrhoids, tympanitis, paralysis, apoplexy, diphtheria and hectic fever. In the 1940s the alternative health practitioner Stanley Burroughs introduced his lemonade, maple syrup and cayenne pepper-based Master Cleanse weight loss and detoxification programme to the United States. Although he was later convicted for practising medicine without a licence, his Master Cleanse is still undertaken by thousands.

Early Uses

The Maya used chillies in the treatment of sore throats and respiratory ailments like coughs and asthma. Although it may seem counterintuitive today, according to the *Libellus de medicinalibus indorum herbis* (Little Book of the Medicinal Herbs of the Indians) of 1552, Aztec physicians recommended chillies for the treatment of such ailments as stomach ulcers and eye infections (administering chilli pepper eye drops!), and prescribed a luxurious face wash of yellow chilli powder mixed with hot urine to combat acne. In Book 10 of his *Historia general*, Bernardino de Sahagún wrote that the Aztec used chillies to combat indigestion, and to ease the pains of childbirth (spicy foods are still commonly recommended as a folk remedy to induce labour). To heal an infected tooth,

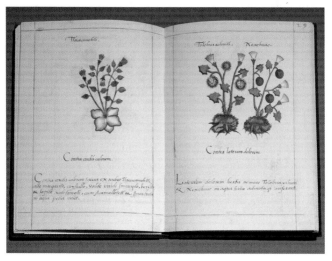

Libellus de medicinalibus indorum herbis (Little Book of the Medicinal Herbs of the Indians), also known as the *Badianus Codex*, written in Nahuatl by the Aztec physician Martinus de la Cruz and translated into Latin by Juannes Badianus (1552).

Sahagún relayed that the cure was a poultice of 'pine resin mixed with ground *conyayaoal* worms', pressed against the tooth with salt and a heated chilli.[2]

Chillies have been adopted by practitioners of other ancient medicines as well. In traditional Chinese medicine they are used as an antiseptic, anti-flatulent and stimulant, to induce perspiration, and to support *yang*. In Indian Ayurvedic medicine chillies are used in similar treatments. Healers in the West Indies used *mandram*, a mixture of cucumbers, chillies, chives, shallots, lime juice and Madeira wine, to stimulate the olfactory system, which, according to one nineteenth-century pharmacopoeia, 'seldom fails to provoke the most languid appetite'.[3]

It was known that chillies could stimulate circulation (as in the treatment of gangrene), but they showed promise as a treatment for virulent disease as well. In the eighteenth century a Grenada physician known only as 'Mr Stewart' wrote a letter to the *Grenada Gazette*, claiming that he had had some success with chillies as a circulation stimulant, and offered up a simple recipe for a pepper sauce made by dissolving chilli paste in vinegar. During a diphtheria outbreak in 1786, which was sweeping the slave population in the West Indies, the British physician John Collins realized that he needed a medicine 'capable of exciting a brisker circulation'. Recalling Stewart's previous letter, Collins decided to try his decoction. He gave the cayenne vinegar to a sick child, and a day later, the scabs inside the boy's throat had already begun to slough off. After continuing the treatment for a few days, the boy made a full recovery, and the chilli vinegar likewise cured every other child who took it.

After the outbreak subsided, Collins documented his findings, writing with excitement that he was 'induced to consider [cayenne] a valuable acquisition' for medicine.[4] Collins offered the caveat that cayenne would probably not solve all cases, and that this particular outbreak had been mild and had been treated swiftly, but this was among the first recorded instances of Western physicians recognizing the medical possibilities of chillies. He also attributed Stewart's knowledge of the efficacy of chillies to the African slaves that had been brought to Grenada by the French and English as early as the seventeenth century.

News spread of the curative properties of capsicums. In the sixth edition of *The Edinburgh New Dispensatory* (1801), cayenne pepper was said to have been effective against 'cachexia Africana', or a wasting syndrome that had been affecting African slaves.[5] As 'one of the simplest and strongest stimulants' that could be eaten, it was effective against 'lethargic affections'.[6] A decade later the physician Andrew Duncan noted that in addition to preventing flatulence from eating vegetables, cayenne had a 'warm and kindly effect in the stomach'.[7] Among those ailments against which chillies were effective, Duncan listed dropsy, coma and delirium, and pinkeye.[8]

Samuel Thomson, a self-taught botanist and herbalist, wrote extensively of the medicinal qualities of chillies, which he claimed to have discovered by accident. In the *New Guide to Health, or Botanic Family Physician*, Thomson recalled that in the autumn of 1800, while searching the mountains of New Hampshire for lady's-slipper orchids, he stopped into a house and marvelled at the *ristra* of cayenne chillies hanging in the room. 'The thought struck me that this might be the article I had so long sought, for the purpose of raising and retaining internal heat', he later recalled.[9]

I knew them to be very hot, but did not know of what nature. I obtained these peppers, carried them home, reduced them to powder, and took some of the powder

Believing that cold was the cause of all illness, Samuel Thomson (1769–1843) wrote extensively on the healing properties of chillies.

myself, and found it to answer the purpose better than any thing else I had made use of.

He mixed the chilli powder with witchhazel tea 'and found that it would retain the heat in the stomach after puking, and preserve the strength of the patient in proportion.'

A few years later, he happened upon bottled cayenne pepper sauce for the first time. He bought some, along with a few dried cayenne chillies, which he added to the bottle. On the way home, he caught a chill, and decided to take a swig from his bottle of hot sauce. It caused 'violent pain for a few minutes, when it produced perspiration', but he quickly felt fine. 'I afterwards tried it, and found that after it had expelled the cold it would not cause pain', he marvelled. 'From these experiments I became convinced that this kind of pepper was much stronger, and would be better for medical use than the common red pepper.'[10] Thus concluded his scientific research, and he began prescribing cayenne as a remedy for a range of maladies. He offered that eating chilli-steeped vinegar aided digestion and cured sores, and noted that a spoonful of the hot sauce 'will remove faint, sinking feelings, which some are subject to, especially in the spring of the year' (possibly referring to Ménière's syndrome or vestibular neuritis – sudden-onset vertigo that is often associated with fatigue, seasonal allergies and respiratory infections).[11]

Thomson's work was well received in anti-elitist, Jacksonian America for its promotion of the idea that, through natural medicines, average people could be in charge of their own health without the help of upper-class doctors. His quaint herbal cures flew in the face of the common medical conventions of the era, which were still reliant on ghastly bloodletting and prescriptions of mercury compounds. Thomson felt that cold was at the root of all illness and promoted raising body heat through steam baths and the liberal use of cayenne. Mid-nineteenth-century dietary reformers like Sylvester Graham and William Andrus Alcott would tend to agree with Thomson's promotion of nutritional healing, but Grahamism was an austere, cold-loving regime that hinged

Postcard advertisement for 'Perry Davis' Vegetable Pain Killer', late 19th century. The medicine's efficacy was derived in part from capsaicin, in addition to opium.

on dense wheat bread and complete abstention from spicy foods. While Graham was deeply worried about the sexually stimulating effects of spices, Alcott warned his readers that they overstimulated the stomach and retarded digestion. This put Grahamites at odds with the laid-back Thomsonians, for whom the stimulation of cayenne was welcome.

Thomson was one of the first Westerners to recommend chilli sauce be applied externally, and other doctors agreed with findings that cayenne was a powerful rubefacient, stimulating blood circulation close to the skin's surface and acting as a useful treatment for chronic rheumatism. The best-selling author Dr Alvin Wood Chase included recipes for cayenne-whiskey liniment in his *Dr Chase's Recipes; or, Information for Everyone* of 1866, and advised drinking a cayenne tea to cure alcoholism (Graham, conversely, insisted that a plain, vegetarian diet would do the trick). Taken three times a day, Chase promised, the stomach and body are toned, 'AND AGAIN YOU FIND YOURSELF A MAN'.[12]

Pain Relief

Samuel Thomson had recommended pepper sauce as a cure for an ailment he called 'ague of the face', known in modern times as trigeminal neuralgia (or Fothergill's disease), a chronic nerve condition characterized by painful facial spasms. Opiates are frequently prescribed to sufferers for the management of the pain, but Thomson instructed that a poultice of cayenne peppers in vinegar be placed inside the mouth, between the teeth and cheek. His is the first recorded case of a physician prescribing topical capsaicin to manage pain, but the analgesic effects of chillies were already well known by Native Americans, who used chilli to manage toothaches.

Chilli powder.

By the 1840s one American innovator, Perry Davis, had launched a national advertising campaign for 'Perry Davis' Vegetable Pain Killer', which was purportedly effective taken either internally or externally. Alvin Wood Chase later published a recipe for the cayenne-based pain killer, noting that it was said to have come from Davis. Mark Twain declared it 'a most detestable medicine', relaying that one taster concluded it was 'made of hellfire'.[13] Davis's miracle elixir relied primarily on opium and ethyl alcohol as its main ingredients, so although its efficacy as a painkiller is undoubted, it is uncertain whether the medicine's burn came from the cayenne or the moonshine.

After having been isolated in increasingly pure forms by nineteenth-century pharmacologists, Hungarians began to lead the way in capsaicin research. Endre Högyes studied the burning effects of pure capsaicin on the mucous membranes and the skin in the late 1800s, and in the early 1900s the professor and organic chemist Tibor Széki was the first to synthesize capsaicin.[14] A decade later, the chemical engineer

Capsicum patches, such as these seen at a Chinese market, are used topically for treating pain.

and plant breeder Ernö Obermayer discovered the scientific basis for capsaicin's pungency: that its production is a stress response in chilli plants (for example, the drier the soils in which it grows, the hotter the chilli).[15] This paved the way for the development of sweeter, less spicy paprika and eventually culminated in Obermayer being awarded Hungary's most prestigious cultural honour, the Kossuth Prize. Széki's later work on the chemistry of anaesthetics in the 1930s led to research in capsaicin's analgesic effects. In the 1960s three Hungarian scientists, Aurelia Jancsó-Gábor, János Pórszász and Nobel Prize nominee Nicolas Jancsó, published their findings that capsaicin activated very specific nerve fibres called nociceptors (aka pain receptors).[16]

This latter discovery led to a manifold increase in research on capsaicin as a tool for pain management. More recently, it was found that in humans, capsaicin (and vanillin) receptors are encoded by the TRPV1 gene, which is also responsible for thermoregulation and the ability to feel pain and scalding sensations. When capsaicin is applied externally, it binds to TRPV1's heat-activated channels, allowing them to fire at a much lower temperature, -37°C, or human body temperature, even though no actual burn damage is occurring. The activation of neurons depletes the body's release of neurotransmitters (effectively overloading the circuits) and desensitizes the body's pain receptors, causing them to mute sensations of discomfort for a period of time.[17]

Unlike the other nightshades, peppers do not contain the toxic, cocaine-like alkaloid tropane; instead, they are armed with the crystalline, heat-producing molecule that affects mammalian mucous membranes with a vibrant quickness. The primary purpose of this morphological feature is to deter mammalian herbivory and fungal infestation, but it is also responsible for the stunning efficacy of pepper spray.

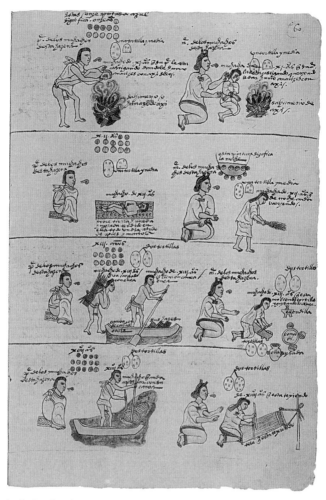

As depicted in the *Codex Mendoza* (*c.* 1535 CE), Aztec parents took extreme measures to keep unruly children in line, including holding the child over chilli smoke.

Chillies as Weapons

During his visit to the Aztec empire in the mid-sixteenth century, the Dominican friar Diego Durán observed the lords of Cuetlaxtla using chillies as a payment of sorts to the tax collectors sent by the king of the neighbouring village. After being given a warm welcome, the tax collectors were invited to relax in a waiting room while the lords fetched the governor. The doors were then locked and the room was pumped full of chilli smoke until the king's messengers all suffocated.[18] (Then, just to drive the point home, the lords of Cuetlaxtla disembowelled the messengers through their anuses, strangled the corpses with their own entrails, used the bodies as dummies in a comedy show and then threw them to the vultures.)

Chilli smoke was similarly used as a fumigant against rats and vermin; in recent toxicity tests, lab rodents were more often killed when overdosed with capsaicin topically than when it had been consumed, but in all cases, the cause of death was determined to be respiratory paralysis. Humans are not as sensitive to capsaicin as mice, but chilli's applications in combat and self-defence have long been of interest outside Mesoamerica. In the Azuchi-Momoyama period during the waning days of feudal Japan, the ninja-blinding devices known as *metsubushi* (sight removers) often relied on chillies. One style, called *sokutoku*, resembled a small box filled with fine sand that had been boiled with chillies. Worn around the neck, the *sokutoku* had a mouthpiece on one end, and a small hole with a plug on the other; when needed, the ninja pulled the plug and blew hard through the mouthpiece, shooting the assailant's eyes with an angry cloud of chilli-coated sand. During the calm and prosperous Edo period, the devices were used by police officers to keep the peace.

Pepper spray being used on protestors by the Seattle Police Department during World Trade Organization protests in 1999.

The type of pepper spray that American civilians might carry was developed in 1960 at the University of Georgia. Originally intended for use as an animal repellent, the oleoresin capsicum (OC) was issued to letter carriers in the U.S. Postal Service in the 1980s so they could ward off dogs during their routes. Wilderness guides around that time began advising that hikers carry it to keep bears or cougars at bay. Although it has been established as an effective deterrent against attackers (human or otherwise), because of its effects on the human respiratory system, pepper spray is illegal for civilian use in most developed countries.

The American government began testing capsaicin as a weapon in 1964, and as recently as 2009 the Indian Armed

Forces began to experiment with weaponized bhut jolokia (aka ghost chilli) in the form of a one-million-Scoville, anti-terrorist tear gas grenade. Chilli's harmful effects are few, but potent; OC-related deaths have even occurred to civilians in police custody. The rush of mucus, sweat and tears ejected from one's face after being assaulted with pepper spray, to some, is not unlike the effects of overdoing it on the sriracha. For many so-called 'chilliheads', that is entirely the point.

5
Chilli Pepper Madness

Upon ingestion of capsaicin, the human brain receives a pain signal and releases opiate-like endorphins, to which one may become addicted. This often leads to a lifetime of gustatory thrill-seeking and Scoville one-upmanship, a characteristic of the so-called 'chillihead'. Chillies were sacred to the Inca, the Maya and the Papago Indians of pre-Columbian Arizona. For the Aztecs, chillies were so central to the diet that to omit them was the definition of fasting. This is the chillihead's code.

Machismo and chilli-pepper-eating competitions have long gone hand in hand. In one episode of the television programme *The Simpsons*, Homer attempts to win such a competition by eating a bowl of chilli that has been doctored with 'the Merciless Peppers of Quetzlzacatenango! Grown deep in the jungle primeval by the inmates of a Guatemalan insane asylum'.[1] He ends up on a mysterious hallucinatory voyage led by his animistic spirit guide, Space Coyote, voiced by 'Ring of Fire' singer Johnny Cash. However, the zenith of macho chilli-eating had already been reached by the Aztec ruler Montezuma when he enjoyed hot sauce as a condiment for the thigh meat of his human sacrifices. Even spies working for Montezuma, if caught in enemy lands, would be killed and eaten with chilli salsa.[2]

Eating the flesh of one's enemies has been an act of bravado for many cultures, including that of several tribes of North American native people. Mexico notwithstanding, chilli-eating out of machismo appears to prevail in cultures with a predominance of milder cuisine. Perhaps it's no coincidence that cultures with milder cuisines have historically controlled cultures with spicier cuisines.

The cultural appropriation of chilli (the meat stew) by white Texans in the late nineteenth century is an example of this; it was a way for Anglo men to reclaim the power compromised by the allure and prowess of the Latina 'Chili Queens'. Chilli cook-offs are still dominated by men. A pot of red-hot chilli is a food a man can cook without jeopardizing his masculinity, because the chilli pepper – an amulet of machismo – protects his manhood. This type of special, or festal, cooking is seen with other foods deemed masculine enough to be prepared by men, such as grilling meats or cooking the occasional heroic pancake breakfast on weekends or holidays. However, in places where chilli-eating is a cultural norm, spicy foods are ferial – everyday foods prepared by the same people that do all the cooking (typically women).

The 'chillihead' phenomenon doesn't appear to exist in cultures for whom chillies are a central part of the cuisine, likely because there is no status to be gained or mettle to be proven from eating them. Among Mexicans, Indians and the Thai people, chilli-eating is not a form of braggadocio, but is tied to early childhood alimentary pedagogy, or the way a child learns to accept his or her cultural diet. The findings of one 2012 study substantiate this, suggesting that frequent exposure to spicy foods is a more reliable predictor of a preference for them than are physiological adaptation or personality differences.[3] There *is* still a different social component to chilli-eating, however; while peer or family pressure features

The Aztec ruler Montezuma II ate the flesh of his human sacrifices with hot sauce.

prominently among the reasons for consuming them, it is through repeated exposure early in life that most children in these cultures acquire a taste (or at least tolerance) for chillies, typically between the ages of four and six.[4] Children become indoctrinated into their family's culinary culture, instead of being relegated to the milder foods reserved for infants.

Besides the fact that it could be one's cultural norm, another reason one might intentionally ingest a food that causes physical pain is that some people genuinely *like* the burning sensation, making it a type of benign masochism.[5] That eating spicy food represents a constrained risk increases its appeal for many – the pain response suggests that eating chillies might be a bit hazardous, but the brain knows there is

Three bowls of chilli lined up to be taste-tested during Sodexo's first Regional Chili Cook-off Competition at Camp Pendleton's 41 Area Mess Hall, 11 May 2010.

Young taster at the 2012 Austin Chronicle Hot Sauce Festival in Austin, Texas.

no real danger (this similarly explains the thrill people derive from bungee jumping or watching horror films). But because repeated exposure decreases both the palate's sensitivity to capsaicin and one's perception of risk, thrill-seeking chilli lovers have little choice but to up the ante, often to ridiculous levels.

In the beginning, though, most Anglos dipped a furtive toe into the world of spicy foods by adding a few specks of cayenne here and there. In 1747 a rather bland curry recipe appeared in Hannah Glasse's *Art of Cookery Made Plain and Easy*, but within fifty years the recipe had added cayenne.[6] The second edition of Amelia Simmons's *American Cookery* (the first American cookbook), published in 1796, features four recipes that include cayenne or 'long pepper' (whole chillies, not *Piper longum*, which had mostly fallen out of use by Simmons's day), one of which is a for a round of beef prepared 'alamode', or in the modern fashion. By the 1803 edition of *Art of Cookery*, the English appreciation for cayenne appears to have caught up with the American; there were about three dozen recipes containing cayenne. Soon, dishes spiked with cayenne got a name that came with a warning of damnation.

What the Devil?

Devilled foods – the heavily seasoned, luxuriously creamy viands seen at picnics and church potlucks – have a long history of being spicy. Though recipes for stuffed eggs existed in the days of Bartolomeo Platina, a fifteenth-century cookbook author in Italy, the use of hot spices like mustard and cayenne in these recipes began in the seventeenth century. The first use of the word 'devilled' can be found in the works of Samuel Johnson's biographer James Boswell, who regularly wrote of eating a supper of 'devilled bones'.[7] With typical recipes of the era calling for marrow bones to be stuffed with butter seasoned with black pepper, a spoonful of mustard and a large pinch of cayenne, it wasn't hard to make the connection between the name and heat.[8] Within a few decades, recipes for all things devilled – chicken, ham, oysters, almonds, tomatoes, lobster, crab, even calves' brains – ran in cookbooks and ladies' magazines. Devilled kidneys on toast became a sensation of the British breakfast table. By the late nineteenth century, the Devil appeared in French dishes served *à la diable*, and in the first half of the twentieth century Italian Americans began serving seafood *fra diavolo*. Nearly every devilled recipe shared one feature: they were kissed with a dash (or more) of chilli.

Some nineteenth-century cookbook authors, like Emma Pike Ewing, clarified that devilled dishes are less heavily sauced than scalloped dishes, that they have a topping of bread or cracker crumbs, and that they are served in bite-sized pieces. It is true that devilled recipes typically call for the food to

Underwood's Original Deviled Ham advertisement, 1905. The red devil is the world's oldest registered trademark.

be finely chopped or mashed, and very often mixed with mayonnaise or white sauce, but a crunchy topping seems to be a matter of taste. Ewing insisted that this was also true of the spices. 'The idea used to obtain that devilled dishes must be intensely hot with seasoning,' Ewing wrote in *The Art of Cookery: A Manual for Homes and Schools* (1891), 'but that idea has been abandoned.'[9] The cookbook author Eneas Sweetland

Dallas was wont to disagree, noting in 1877 that 'a moderate devil is almost a contradiction in terms', and Frances Emugene Owens was more vehement in her dissent, writing in her *New Cook Book and Complete Household Manual* (1897) that, make no mistake, 'devilled means very hot'.[10]

Devilled kidneys, in particular, may have got a bad rap not just for being spicy, but because, through no fault of their own, they happened to pair perfectly with alcohol. One nineteenth-century writer noted that unlike an *apéritif* such as lettuce, which was not an effective excuse for drinking after dinner, 'something hot and well spiced . . . like our devilled kidneys and grilled bones, would be more likely to effect that delightful object'.[11] By dint of their luxury, devilled kidneys somehow became a symbol of the aristocracy, and a trope for pomposity in literature.[12] One of the most humorous of Edgar Allan Poe's criticisms of the novel *Charles O'Malley, The Irish Dragoon* (written in 1841 by Poe's arch-rival Charles Lever, and in which 'there are more absurdities than we have patience to enumerate') was that the novel mentioned devilled kidneys too many times.[13] 'And then we have one unending, undeviating succession of junketings, in which "devilled kidneys" are never by any accident found wanting', he carped.[14] 'The truth is, that drinking, telling anecdotes, and devouring "devilled kidneys" may be considered as the sum total, as the *thesis* of the book.'[15] As if that's a bad thing.

Some Like it Hot

Even in dishes not named after the Dark Lord himself, chillies have been the subject of a number of cultural taboos. Ritual fasting among the Maya always required the elimination of chillies along with salt, and the Kashmiri pandits or Brahmins

Trafalgar Dinner.

VINS.

—

FINE OLD SOLERA.

LIEBFRAUMILCH, 1884.
(S. FRIEDBORIG'S.)

G. H. MUMM & CO'S,
EXTRA QUALITY, EXTRA
DRY, 1892.
DUMINY & CO,
EXTRA QUALITY,
EXTRA DRY, 1889.

LIQUEURS VARIÉES.

CHÂTEAU
MOUTON ROTHSCHILD, 1889
FEUERHEERD'S PORT,
COMMENDADOR.
25 YEARS OLD.

THE GRAND HOTEL, LONDON.

Potages.
Consommé Dauphine.
Crème d'Asperges.

Poissons.
Filets de Soles à la Navy.
Blanchailles à la Diable.

Entrées.
Ortolans en Chaudfroid.
Côtelettes de Pré-salé aux Haricots verts.

Grosses Pièces.
Contre-filets piqués à la Flamande.
Jambon au Champagne.

Rôti.
Faisans bardés à la Broche.
Salade Cœurs de Chicorée.
Pommes de Terre Copeaux.

Entremets.
Poudings Mousselines à la Gourmet.
Plombière glacé à la Grand Hôtel.
Petites Friandises.

Relevé.
Croquettes de Fromage à la Diable.

—

Dessert et Café Noir.

OCTOBER 21ST, 1897.

A menu for a special event dinner held in 1897 at the Grand Hotel in London illustrates the popularity of devilled dishes such as whitebait (listed as *Blanchailles à la Diable*).

(the priest and yogi caste) of India avoid strong flavours, believing that spicy foods are bad for the *dosha* (humours) and provoke negativity. Those with high amounts of the *pitta dosha*, or bilious humours, whose chief quality is heat, are purportedly especially susceptible to aggression if chillies and other pungent foods form too great a portion of the diet. For other cultures, the objection to eating chillies was more prudish: spicy foods inflame passions.

Spicy foods have been historically linked to venereal fervour, possibly because of their properties as a stimulant. Observations made by the Spanish archbishop Pedro de Villagómez in the seventeenth century suggest that even the ancient Peruvians likened the fire of chillies to the burn of sexual desire. During the six-day harvest festival celebrating the ripening of the avocado trees, men abstained from both chillies and sex, and the festival concluded with a nude footrace and copulation in the streets.[16] Hungarians, too, correlate a woman's tolerance of paprika with her sexual appetite, and one rare heirloom *C. annuum* variety called the 'Peter pepper' takes a more literal approach by bearing an uncanny resemblance to a circumcised penis.

Physicians in the mid-nineteenth century wrote about the aphrodisiac effects of chillies. Although the physician Alfred Stillé took a jab at Samuel Thomson in his *Therapeutics and Materia Medica* (1860), mocking his free use of capsicum as 'quackery', he did concede that capsicum was entitled 'to be ranked among the aphrodisiacs'.[17] Roberts Bartholow wrote in no uncertain terms that capsicum produced excellent results against impotence, and that 'decided aphrodisiac effects are produced by red pepper'.[18] These are presumably garnered from the ingestion of chillies, rather than applying them directly to one's genitals.

These findings came after a few decades of pulpit-beating about the dangers of eating chillies. Bedevilling food was

The suggestive form of this *C. annuum* cultivar has earned it the name 'Peter pepper'.

considered not just unhealthy but 'highly injurious' by the nineteenth-century hygienist and staunch masturbation opponent Sylvester Graham. Along with alcohol, caffeine, meat and sex, spices were among those things he held accountable for 'blunting and destroying' the organs, and from which 'rigid self-denial' could cure all ills.[19] 'All kinds of stimulating and heating substances', he blustered, 'high-seasoned food . . . more or less – and some to a very great degree – increase the concupiscent excitability and sensibility of the genital organs . . . and on the intellectual and moral faculties.'[20] He called fiery seasonings 'some of the most powerful of the class of artificial stimulants' and warned good Christians against them.[21]

Graham perhaps had a point; the heat from chillies had been accused of being overstimulating in more ways than one, even after his time. Connections between machismo and chilli-eating were exposed in the late nineteenth-century hazing rituals of West Point Naval Academy cadets. In 1898 the cadet Oscar Booz was forced to drink Tabasco sauce or face a beating. Booz dropped out of school four months later and died the following year of tubercular laryngitis – a condition for which his family blamed the effects of the Tabasco *gavage*. They took legal action against the school, but the expert witness, Dr Jacob da Silva Solis-Cohen (the nation's first head and neck surgeon), cleared the Tabasco of all wrongdoing.[22] And in 1970 Peru prisons suffered a rash of sexual offences, leading the Peruvian government to ban hot sauce from the prisoners' diet. Policymakers were so convinced of the aphrodisiac effects of chillies that they worried that 'men forced to live a limited lifestyle' would turn to homosexuality if inflamed by chilli-induced passions while stuck behind bars.[23]

In late nineteenth-century America there emerged an opinion that spicy foods were 'barbarous', and not to be relished by proper people. A little chilli pepper was fine, but 'only the lower classes use it in excess', cautioned the Catholic priest Augustine Francis Hewit.[24] In actuality it is merely those with a preference for spicy foods who use chilli in excess, though it was nothing new for some members of society to criticize those who enjoyed stimulation. The supposition that spiciness is a preference of boorish extroverts is unsupported by scientific evidence, though; as mentioned, it is merely exposure that leads to a taste for the spice. Because tolerance to heat does build over time, benign *pico de gallo* and fried jalapeño poppers really are like the gateway drugs to a more potent experience. For those craving that delicious burn, the only solution is more Scovilles.

It started fairly recently. Some American GIs returned from the Vietnam War with a newly formed taste for chillies. In the late 1970s, recalled Dave DeWitt, most chilliheads were macho, middle-aged men engaged in chilli-eating pissing contests.[25] Soon, however, chilliheads came to include immigrants hailing from chilli-eating countries, homesick for full-throttle heat. Chinese tourism didn't begin until the 1980s, a few years after China opened its doors to foreigners and the construction of hotels and airports began in earnest. The 1990s saw a spike in foreign travel to Thailand, and tourists returned home with newly formed tolerances for pungency.[26] The rise of the chilliheads was at hand.

Salsa Brava

Repugnant hot sauce names like Dr Assburn's Fire-Roasted Habanero Pepper Sauce, Professor Phardtpounder's Colon Cleaner! and Screaming Sphincter Cayenne Sauce do little to dissuade critics about what kind of person prefers excess spice. Reaper Squeezins is made with a pepper called Carolina Reaper, created by the self-proclaimed mad scientist 'Smokin' Ed Currie, while crossing sweet habanero and naga viper chillies; with 1,569,300 SHU, this is the world's hottest (as of February 2015).[27] Other sauces like 'Satan's Blood', 'Liquid Lucifer' or 'Hell Devil's Revenge', warn of the eschatonic fate of those who deign to eat it. Un-Christian though they may sound, these sauce names aren't meant to draw a mainstream crowd. Quite the opposite. Like the red and black ventrum of a fire-belly toad, they are a warning to the hapless and a beacon to the like-minded.

Most people, however, are content with eating foods sauced with something milder than a million Scovilles. By the time upper-class diners were raising an eyebrow about precisely how much chilli polite society should reasonably consume, Tabasco-brand sauce (2,500–5,000 SHU) had already been in production for three decades. In the American South a dash of Tabasco sauce was all that was needed to spice up a humdrum mutton roast or poached eggs, and it perked up pimento cheese, salad dressings and pickles. Even at the Boston Cooking School, Tabasco sauce was the devil in devilled chestnuts.

During the years following the American Civil War the dietary habits of Southerners took a rather bland turn (due in no small part to the fact that they no longer had skilled slaves to do the cooking or farming). Setting out to solve this, an enterprising Louisiana banker named Edmund McIlhenny founded the Tabasco brand in 1868, beginning with a sauce made from chillies that had been salted and fermented for a month. After thirty days, the chilli mash, now somewhat resembling a spicy sour pickle relish, was blended with white wine vinegar and aged for another month to mellow it. After straining and corking the sauce into little cologne bottles, McIlhenny began marketing his sauce around the southeastern U.S. By 1870 he not only had a patent but had begun shipping Tabasco sauce all over the U.S. and across the pond to the UK.

Other American sauces followed: Frank's RedHot (1920), still the gold standard for saucing Buffalo chicken wings; Crystal Hot Sauce (1923) and Original Louisiana Hot Sauce (1928), both made in Louisiana and each effective at improving a humble pot of gumbo or plate of grits; and Texas Pete (1929), which was, despite the moniker, born at a North Carolina barbecue stand.

Bottled Mexican taco sauces like Cholula, Valentina's, El Yucateca and Tapatío, as well as Mexican-style American salsas like Pace and Old El Paso, are a more recent phenomenon, coming into commercial production in the 1950s and '60s – around the same time as Mexican restaurants began opening in parts of the U.S. north of Los Angeles. There are several reasons they came out so late: first, homemade salsa was readily available in every Mexican household, and most Americans couldn't take the heat of more piquant sauces. Second, most Americans didn't have a way to eat salsa; there wasn't a very large market for bottled sauces in the United States until the invention of the burrito and the release of tortillas and corn chips into mainstream American grocery stores.

The fast-food chain Taco Bell played no small role in cultivating the nation's adoration of hot sauce, particularly once it began selling franchises outside of California in the 1960s. In early Mexican American restaurants (which was the only place most non-Latino Americans ate Mexican food), one only had to ask for the sauce on one's food; 'dinners prepared with hot sauce at request, no extra charge' was a frequent promise on menus.[28]

Today, hot sauce has such a profound following that it is now found in a number of places where it perhaps has

Hot sauces with sinister names seen in San Diego, California.

Sriracha sauces from Asia and the United States. American interest in spicy foods rose after veterans returned from the Vietnam War in the early 1970s.

no business. Frank's RedHot-flavoured Pringles crisps and Tapatío-flavoured Doritos aren't out of the realm of sanity, but Tabasco-flavoured Jelly Belly jelly beans, Hot Japanese Chilli KitKat chocolate bars, Rogue Brewery's sriracha-flavoured stout beer and several brands of novelty drinks illustrate the absurd heights to which enthusiasts will take their passion for peppers.

Dessert

As strange as it may seem today, mixing chillies with sweets or beverages is hardly new. Chillies graced the drinking chocolate that was reserved for the rulers and warriors of the Aztec empire; honey, vanilla and various aromatic spices tempered

Borden's pimento cheese spread.

the heat nicely. (Noblewomen, who ate separately and for whom cacao was off-limits, enjoyed a dessert of chia gruel sprinkled with chilli instead.) Spaniards balked in disgust at the thick and frothy beverage, sputtering that the consistency and crimson colour, derived from ground annatto seeds, made the chocolate look like blood.[29] The spicy complexity of the chocolate beverage went completely over European heads, but the Aztecs were onto something. 'Combining sugar with spice is the pinnacle of refined palates', explained the humourist Gustavo Arellano in *Ask a Mexican*, and this notion is exemplified by the wide range of high-end, small-batch, chilli-laced chocolates available today.[30]

Spicy sweets didn't take hold in the United States until centuries later. In the 1930s the candy company Ferrara-Pan introduced the cinnamon-flavoured Red Hots, and became the first candy maker to connect cassia (cinnamon) flavour to tongue-tingling spice. Twenty years later they introduced Atomic Fireballs, whose nuclear heat comes from capsaicin. With the help of the pop-culture obsession with mushroom clouds, the spicy candy quickly made its way into mainstream American culture. A wave of other spicy cinnamon candies followed: Just Born's Hot Tamales, Brach's Cinnamon Disks and Sweet's Cinnamon Bears all launched to the glee of baby boomer children. But despite the Scots' preference for strong flavours and a long English history of spice-flavoured comfits, pungent cinnamon sweets have never been very popular in the UK.[31]

We humans have taken a pungent red berry and enmeshed it into nearly every aspect of our culture. In only a few hundred years – a hummingbird's heartbeat, in the scale of human evolution – chillies have come to not just punctuate, but define, much of the world's cuisine. The fact that the mammalian body is physiologically designed to feel the pain of chillies is the plant's doing. But the fact that the human mammal comes back for more punishment is our own fault. An appreciation for chillies is not just built into the human body; it's human nature.

Appendix: When Pa Firs' Et Tabasco Sauce

Alfred James Waterhouse (1899)

When pa firs' et Tabasco sauce – I'm smilin' bout
   it yet,
Although his subsekent remarks I always shall regret.
We'd come to town to see the sights, an' pa remarked
   to me:
'We'll eat at a bong tong hotel an' sling some style,'
   says he.
An' then he sort o' cast his eye among the plates an' all,
An' says, 'That ketchup mus' be good; the bottle is so small;'
An' then he took a piece of meat an' covered it quite thick,
When pa firs' et Tabasco sauce an' rose to make his kick.

It all comes back so plain to me; I rikollect it well;
He just was talkin' mild an' calm, an' then he give a yell
An' tried to cave the ceilin' in by buttin' with his head.
'Er-hooh! Er-hooh! Fire! Murder! Hooh!' I can't tell all
   he said,
But when they heard his heated words six women lef'
   the room
An' said such language filled their souls with shame an'
   also gloom,

But pa he only gurgled some, an' then he yelled again,
When firs' he et Tabasco sauce an' told about it then.

We laid him out upon a board an' fanned him quite a while,
An' pa he sort o' gasped at firs' an' then he tried to smile,
An' says: 'Jus' heat a poker now an' run it down my neck –
I want to cool off gradual; it's better, I expeck.'
But when he got me out o' doors, he says: 'I want to get
Thet there blame ketchup's recipe an' learn jes' how it's het,
So I can try it on the boys when you an' me git hum,
Till they, too, think the condiment is mixed with Kingdom
    Come.'

I've told the story, but I guess perhaps I oughtn't to,
Fer pa don't go with me no more, the way he used to do.
He said some words, of course I know, that were too
    sizzlin' hot,
But still I hope up where he's gone they're all of them
    forgot.
An' if they ain't per'aps my pa will to the angels say:
'I wish you'd try that ketchup stuff I et down there that
    day.'
Of course I feel they can't approve, but I hope, just
    the same,
If once they eat Tabasco sauce they'll count him less
    to blame.

Recipes

Historical Recipes

Pimento Cheese

Martha McCulloch-Williams, *Dishes & Beverages of the Old South* (1913)

The author's version of this classic Southern American spread relies on a half-cup of homemade mayonnaise instead of French dressing, and a few handfuls of shredded sharp cheddar cheese in addition to just one brick of cream cheese. Adding a clove of minced garlic, a teaspoon of smoked paprika and a few teaspoons of dill pickle juice in addition to the jarred pimento (or pickled sweet-hot cherry peppers) also helps brighten things up. By 1911 packaged pimento cheese was available in American grocery stores as far from the South as Portland, Oregon. Serve with saltines and celery sticks.

Make the pimento cheese by grinding fine half a can of pimento, and mixing it through two cakes of cream cheese, softening the cheese with French dressing, and seasoning it to taste.
Makes about 2 1/2 cups (120 ml)

Chilli con Carne

This is the original San Antonio Chili Queens' Recipe (*c.* 1890s), from the South Texas Heritage Center.

2 lbs beef shoulder, cut into ½-inch cubes
1 lb pork shoulder, cut into ½-inch cubes
¼ cup suet
¼ cup pork fat
3 medium-sized onions, chopped
6 garlic cloves, minced
1-quart water
4 ancho chillies
1 serrano chilli
6 dried red chillies
1 tablespoon cumin seeds, freshly ground
2 tablespoons Mexican oregano
salt to taste

Place lightly floured beef and pork cubes in with suet and pork fat in heavy chilli pot and cook quickly, stirring often. Add onions and garlic and cook until they are tender and limp. Add water to mixture and simmer slowly while preparing chillies. Remove stems and seeds from chilli and chop very finely. Grind chillies in molcajete (mortar and pestle) and add oregano with salt to mixture. Simmer another two hours. Remove suet casing and skim off.

Chiles Rellenos
Encarnación Pinedo, *Encarnación's Kitchen* (1898)

One would be hard-pressed to find a more straightforward recipe, but there are nine others in the cookbook with varying fillings and levels of complexity.

Use poblano chillies and a white cheese such as Monterey Jack, and serve with warm tomato salsa. Slice the cheese not too thin and stuff the chillies; roll them in egg and fry them.

Duck Vindaloo

Navroji Framji, *Indian Cookery 'Local' for Young Housekeepers* (1887)

Have a large fat duck, and after it is well washed in water, dry it well in a clean towel, and wash it again in weak vinegar. Cut it in pieces as for curry. Grind into paste with vinegar on a clean well dried stone the same mussala as is used in Frithath Curry No. 196 [recipe follows], and cut in slices green ginger and garlic; determine the quantity of mussala by the size of the duck. Rub the pieces of duck well with 2/3 of the mussala, lay the pieces in a large bowl, and strew over each layer a little fine salt and a portion of ginger and garlic. Pour over the whole good vinegar, cover the bowl and let it stand for 6 or 8 hours. Warm 6 oz. of ghee, or ¾ of a tea cup of mustard oil, fry the remaining mussala, then add to it the duck, mussala and vinegar in the bowl, cook the curry in an earthenware chatty on a slow fire for two hours. When cold, place the curry in a jar or bottle. The vinegar and oil must cover the meat. No water must be used in the preparation of vindaloo.

Frithath Curry

Navroji Framji, *Indian Cookery 'Local' for Young Housekeepers* (1887)

This is a very hot curry, too hot for most people. Materials 1 lb. of Beef, a table spoon of ghee, one onion, 3 pods of tamarind and 3 or 4 table spoons of vinegar. The curry stuff to be ground with vinegar. Half a tea spoon of jeera [cumin], 8 or 10 corns of pepper, 6 red chillies, two inches of turmeric, 4 cloves, 5 cardomons and 2 inches of cinnamon. Cut four green chillies down the centre, ten cloves of garlic and ¼ ounce green ginger into slices. Directions. Put the ghee in a chatty on the fire, warm it and fry a cut onion, also the green chillies, ginger and garlic slightly. Add the meat cut up as usual, cover the pan and let it cook in the ghee. Have a good fire or your meat will get tough by the extraction of its juices. Shake occasionally to prevent it burning. When the gravy evaporates and the ghee appears, add the curry paste (reduce your fire) and let it brown till it gives out a pleasant smell. Be careful that it does not burn. Lastly add the curry stuff water and a tea cup of water. Extract the juice of the tamarind with three desert (*sic*) spoons of vinegar. Add this to the curry, simmer gently till ready. Omit the onion if the curry is wanted for the day following. Add the acid gradually lest the curry should be made too sour.

Modern Recipes

Curried Devilled Egg Salad Sandwiches

Devilled egg salad sandwiches are less fiddly to make than devilled eggs, and they can still be sliced into quarters and wrapped in tidy wax paper for a pretty picnic presentation. Alternatively, the recipe may be used for superlative curried devilled eggs.

Hard boil five eggs, crack them gently all over and peel them under running water. Halve each lengthwise and pop out the creamy yolks into a bowl. You want these to be particularly devilish, so in addition to two tablespoons of mayonnaise, add a tablespoon of jalapeño mustard and a teaspoon each of hot paprika and curry powder, plus a few pinches of salt and pepper, a couple dashes of smoky *pimentón dulce* and a dash of mustard powder. Next add a tablespoon each of parsley, pickled onions (preferably homemade) and sweet-hot jarred peppadews (or cherry peppers), each minced finely. Blend the yolk mixture with a fork until smooth, then add the whites, coarsely chopped. Smear a slice of bread with mayonnaise, add a handful of shredded iceberg lettuce and spoon on about two and a half eggs' worth of the devilled egg salad. Sprinkle on another dash

of hot paprika for good measure, add the other slice of bread, and
devour the sandwich standing at your kitchen counter.
Makes 2 sandwiches

Harissa

This North African condiment is sublime on grilled fish, or stirred
into pilafs and stews.

8 dried guajillo chillies
3 dried ancho chillies
3 dried chipotle chillies
3 sun-dried tomatoes (not in oil)
½ tsp caraway seeds
¼ tsp coriander seeds
¼ tsp cumin seeds
1 tsp dried mint leaves
1 roasted red bell pepper, seeded (jarred is fine)
3 tbsp extra-virgin olive oil, plus more as needed
1 ½ tsp sea or kosher salt
4 cloves garlic
juice of 1 lemon

Remove the stems and seeds from the dried chillies; if you
have sensitive skin, it's best to wear gloves, or at least wash your
hands immediately. Put the chillies and sun-dried tomatoes into a
medium bowl, cover with boiling water and let sit until softened,
about twenty minutes. Meanwhile, toast the caraway, coriander
and cumin in a small skillet over medium heat until very fragrant,
swirling constantly to prevent burning (this takes about a minute).
Transfer the spices to a grinder or a mortar and pestle with the
dried mint and grind finely.

Drain the chillies and tomatoes, and transfer to a food pro-
cessor with the spices and remaining ingredients. Purée, scraping
down the sides of the bowl occasionally and adding more olive oil
as needed until the paste reaches a smooth, velvety consistency.

Scrape into a pint jar and top off with about 1 cm of oil. Store in the refrigerator up to three weeks, adding more oil after each use.
Makes 1 cup (225 ml)

Hungarian Gulyás

1 tbsp lard or oil
1 medium onion, diced
½ tsp crushed caraway seed
2 tbsp noble-sweet Hungarian paprika
1 lb (500 g) beef chuck, cubed
salt and pepper to taste
1 quart (1 litre) water
2 large potatoes, cubed

Heat lard or oil in a Dutch oven (or large, thick-bottomed pot) and sauté the onions over medium heat until translucent. Add the paprika and caraway, stir, then add the beef, and a few pinches of salt and pepper. Brown the meat on all sides, then add the water and bring to a simmer. Turn the heat to low and simmer, covered, for about 30 minutes. Add the potatoes, salt and pepper, adding more water as needed to cover the potatoes. Simmer another 10–15 minutes or until potatoes are tender. Correct seasoning to your palate.
Serves 6

Shakshouka

This satisfying egg dish makes a lovely breakfast for three, or add a salad for a light supper for four. If one were to add fried corn tortillas (or even stale tortilla chips), sprinkle with crumbled cotija cheese and a small handful of minced coriander leaves, this comes close to traditional Mexican *chilaquiles*.

3 tbsp olive oil
1 small onion, sliced

2 garlic cloves, minced
1 red bell pepper, sliced finely
750 g chopped tomatoes, preferably fire-roasted
¼ tsp smoked paprika
¼ tsp Aleppo pepper (or Turkish paprika)
2 tsp ground cumin
½ tsp ground coriander
½ tsp harissa (more if you like heat) or cayenne
¼ tsp turmeric powder
1 tsp salt
½ tsp freshly ground black pepper
6 eggs

In a large frying pan or saucepan, fry the onions, garlic and peppers in olive oil until they become glossy and soft, about ten minutes on medium-high heat. Add the spices and stir, cooking for about two minutes to release the oils. Add the tomatoes and simmer for about an hour, or until the onions and peppers are very soft (your patience will be rewarded). Add a splash of water here and there to make sure the sauce doesn't burn. Crack in the eggs and let them simmer for about five minutes, or until the whites have set, but the yolks are still a bit squidgy. Alternatively (if making *menemen*), dribble in whisked eggs and cook until set. Serve with warm flatbread and a sprinkle of parsley and coriander.
Serves 3–4

Kung Pao Chicken

This is loosely adapted from Fuchsia Dunlop's recipe. Although it isn't traditional, diced celery is a welcome addition.

5 boneless chicken thighs or 2 boneless chicken breasts (or a combination, for about a half kilo of meat)
¼ cup (110 ml) peanut oil
15–20 dried red chillies, preferably Sichuanese 'facing heaven' chillies
1 tsp Sichuan peppercorns
4 cloves of garlic, minced
2 tbsp fresh ginger, minced
4 Chinese garlic chives or 2 spring onions (scallions), cut into 3-cm lengths (reserve some, finely sliced, for garnish)
¾ cup (110 g) roasted unsalted peanuts

For the marinade:
½ tsp salt
2 tsp light soy sauce
1 tsp Shaoxing rice wine or medium-dry sherry
4 tsp arrowroot starch or 2¼ tsp cornflour
1 tsp water

For the sauce:
3 tsp sugar
2 tsp arrowroot starch or 1⅛ tsp cornflour
1 tsp each dark and light soy sauce
3 tsp Zhenjiang (Chinese black) vinegar (may substitute a mix of aged balsamic and rice vinegar)
1 tsp sesame oil
1 tsp chicken stock or water

Cut the chicken evenly into roughly 1-cm cubes, place it in a bowl and mix in the marinade ingredients. While the chicken is marinating, snip the chillies in half lengthwise and shake out and discard the seeds. Lightly crush the Sichuan peppercorns with a mortar and pestle, and get the sauce ready by combining the ingredients in a small bowl.

Heat the oil over a high flame, and when it's hot (but not yet smoking) add the chillies and Sichuan peppercorns. Stir-fry briefly until they are crisp and the oil is spicy and fragrant, but don't let them burn. Push them to the edges of the wok, then add the chicken and stir-fry over a high flame. Cook for one minute, stirring constantly, then add the ginger, garlic and spring onions. Stir-fry for a few minutes until the chicken is nearly cooked. Toss in the peanuts, stir-fry for about 30 seconds, then give the sauce a quick stir and pour it in. Toss everything together, and cook for about 30 seconds, or until the sauce is thickened and glossy. Sprinkle with finely sliced spring onions and serve with steamed white rice.

Serves 2 as a main dish with a simple stir-fried vegetable and rice, or 4 as part of a family-style Chinese meal with other dishes.

Nam Pla Prik (Thai Chilli Dipping Sauce)

This basic condiment is seen on every Thai table.

3–5 Thai chillies, preferably a mix of green and red, thinly sliced
crosswise, with seeds
2 tbsp good quality Thai fish sauce
1 tbsp freshly squeezed lime juice
½ tsp palm sugar

Combine all the ingredients.
Makes about ¼ cup (50 ml)

Kimchi Jjigae (Korean Kimchi Stew)

This is how Korean housewives use up kimchi that's too ripe to eat on its own.

For the anchovy stock:
1,350 ml (6 cups) water
15 g (about ½ cup) dried anchovies
1 piece of kombu seaweed (kelp), about 3 cm by 5 cm
3 dried shiitake mushrooms
Note: For a richer version, meat broth may be substituted, or use a combination of anchovy and meat broth.

For the soup:
6 cups (1.4 kg) kimchi (older/riper kimchi is more traditional)
2 tsp sesame oil
55 ml (¼ cup) mirin (sweet rice wine)
4 spring onions, sliced thinly
Add-ons: 1 package firm tofu, sliced; cooked beef or pork, sliced thinly; prawns, scallops or canned tuna; 4 eggs
Optional condiments: sesame oil, *doenjang, gochujang*

Make anchovy stock by bringing the water to the boil, adding the anchovies, kombu and shiitake, and then simmering over a medium heat for ten minutes. Strain and return to the pot to simmer over medium-high heat (and/or heat the meat broth, if using).

Strain the kimchi juice into the stock, slice the kimchi into shreds, then add to the stock along with the sesame oil and mirin. Simmer for five minutes. After the stew has simmered for five minutes, add the tofu, meats and/or seafood (but not the egg) and simmer for another five minutes, or until everything is warmed through. When everything is bubbly, carefully crack in the eggs and gently poach them for one minute.

Divide the stew into four servings (taking care not to break the yolks), and then top each bowl with a generous pinch of spring onions. Serve with bowls of steamed rice, and pass around sesame oil, *doengjang* and/or *gochujang* for extra umami and flavour.
Serves 4

References

Introduction

1 Ann Bingham, *South and Meso-American Mythology A to Z* (New York, 2004), p. 74.
2 Alan Davidson, *Food in Motion: The Migration of Foodstuffs and Cookery Techniques*, vol. 1 (Proceedings of 1983 Oxford Symposium) (Oxford, 1983), p. 139.

1 Taxonomy and Ecology

1 Albert Brown Lyons, *Practical Standardization by Chemical Assay of Organic Drugs and Galenicals* (Detroit, MI, 1920), p. 238.
2 Ivette Guzman, Paul W. Bosland and Mary A. O'Connell, 'Heat, Colour, and Flavour Compounds in Capsicum Fruit', in *The Biological Activity of Phytochemicals*, ed. David Gang (New York, 2011), p. 117.
3 Lyons, *Practical Standardization*, p. 238.
4 Ibid.
5 Joshua J. Tewksbury et al., 'Evolutionary Ecology of Pungency in Wild Chilies', *Proceedings of the National Academy of Sciences of the United States of America* (19 August 2008), p. 11808.
6 Paul W. Sherman and Jennifer Billing, 'Darwinian

Gastronomy: Why We Use Spices', *BioScience*, XLIX/6 (1999), pp. 453–63.

7 Paul W. Sherman and Jennifer Billing, 'Antimicrobial Functions of Spice: Why Some Like it Hot', *Quarterly Review of Biology*, LXXIII/1 (March 1998), pp. 3–49.

8 Jean Andrews Smith, *Peppers: The Domesticated Capsicums* (Austin, TX, 1984), p. 114.

9 Amit Krishna De, *Capsicum: The Genus Capsicum* (London, 2003), p. 2.

2 American Roots

1 Paul E. Minnis and Michael E. Whalen, 'The First Prehispanic Chili "(Capsicum)" from the U.S. Southwest/Northwest Mexico and Its Changing Use', *American Antiquity*, LXXV/2 (April 2010), pp. 245–57.

2 Araceli Aguilar-Meléndez et al., 'Genetic Diversity and Structure in Semiwild and Domesticated Chilies (*Capsicum annuum*; Solanaceae) From Mexico', *American Journal of Botany*, XCV/6 (2009), pp. 1190–202.

3 Theresa Hill et al., 'Characterization of *Capsicum annuum* Genetic Diversity and Population Structure Based on Parallel Polymorphism Discovery with a 30K Unigene Pepper GeneChip', *PLoS ONE*, VIII/2 (February 2013), http://journals.plos.org.

4 Jared Diamond, *Guns, Germs and Steel* (New York, 1999), p. 188.

5 Kraig H. Kraft et al., 'Multiple Lines of Evidence for the Origin of Domesticated Chili Pepper, *Capsicum annuum*, in Mexico', *Proceedings of the National Academy of Science*, CXI/17 (29 April 2014), pp. 6165–70.

6 Paul W. Bosland, Eric J. Votava and Eric M. Votava, *Peppers: Vegetable and Spice Capsicums* (Boston, MA, 2012), p. 2.

7 Minnis and Whalen, 'The First Prehispanic Chili "(Capsicum)" from the U.S. Southwest/Northwest Mexico and Its Changing Use', pp. 245–57.

8 Ann Bingham and Jeremy Roberts, *South and Meso-American Mythology A to Z* (New York, 2010), p. 57.

9 Marina Warner and Felipe Fernández-Armesto, *World of Myths* (Austin, TX, 2004), vol. II, pp. 358–9.

10 David Adams Leeming, *Creation Myths of the World: Parts I–II* (Santa Barbara, CA, 2010), p. 141.

11 Ker Than, 'Machu Picchu Is Mini Re-creation of a Mythic Landscape?', *National Geographic News,* 15 June 2009, http://news.nationalgeographic.com.

12 Frances Berdan and Patricia Rieff Anawalt, *The Essential Codex Mendoza* (Berkeley, CA, 1997), pp. 161–2.

13 Diego Álvarez Chanca, *Letter of Dr Chanca on the Second Voyage of Columbus* (Madison, WI, 2003), pp. 311–12, www.americanjourneys.org.

14 Edward Gaylord Bourne, *The Voyages of Columbus and of John Cabot* (New York, 1906), p. 227.

15 David DeWitt, *Precious Cargo: How Foods from the Americas Changed the World* (Berkeley, CA, 2014), p. 28.

16 Minnis and Whalen, 'The First Prehispanic Chile ("Capsicum") from the U.S. Southwest/Northwest Mexico and its Changing Use', pp. 245–58.

17 Erna Fergusson, *Mexican Cookbook* (Albuquerque, NM, 2011), Kindle edition.

18 Fabian Garcia, 'Improved Variety No. 9 of Native Chile', *Bulletin: Agricultural Experiment Station, New Mexico College of Agriculture and Mechanic Arts,* Issue 124 (Las Cruces, NM, 1920), p. 16.

19 Amelia Simmons, *American Cookery* (Hartford, CT, 1798), pp. 21–3.

20 Jules Arthur Harder, *The Physiology of Taste: Harder's Book of Practical American Cookery* (San Francisco, CA, 1885), vol. I, p. 256.

21 Technically, there is a species of walnut endemic to California (*Juglans californica*), but its ethnobotanical use appears to have been limited to the Chumash people of the southern California coast.

22 Jeffrey M. Pilcher, *Planet Taco: A Global History of Mexican Food* (New York, 2013), p. 30.

3 Worldwide Adoption

1 Edward G. Bourne, ed., 'Original Narratives of the Voyages of Columbus', in *The Northmen: Columbus and Cabot, 985–1503* (New York, 1906), pp. 227–8, at www.gutenberg.org.

2 David DeWitt, *Precious Cargo: How Foods from the Americas Changed the World* (Berkeley, CA, 2014), p. 23.

3 John Gerard, *Herball; or, Generall Historie of Plantes* (London, 1597), pp. 365–6, at https://archive.org.

4 Ibid., p. 366.

5 Jean Andrews Smith, *Peppers: The Domesticated Capsicums* (Austin, TX, 1984), p. 23.

6 DeWitt, *Precious Cargo*, p. 86.

7 Mark Kurlansky, *Cod: A Biography of the Fish That Changed the World* (New York, 1998), p. 267.

8 Zoltán Halász, *Hungarian Paprika Through the Ages* (Budapest, 1963), p. 24.

9 DeWitt, *Precious Cargo*, p. 83.

10 Joanne Sasvari, *Paprika: A Spicy Memoir from Hungary* (Toronto, 2005), pp. 59–60.

11 Ibid., p. 202.

12 Johann Georg Kohl, *Austria: Vienna, Prague, Hungary, Bohemia and the Danube; Galicia, Styria, Moravia, Bukovina and the Military Frontier* (London, 1843), p. 182.

13 R. N. Lester and A. Seck, 'Solanum aethiopicum L. [Internet] Record from PROTA4U', in PROTA *(Plant Resources of Tropical Africa / Ressources végétales de l'Afrique tropicale)*, ed. G.J.H. Grubben and O. A. Denton (Wageningen, Netherlands, 2004), www.prota4u.org, accessed 12 January 2015.

14 Maryn McKenna, 'How the Syrian Conflict Affects Your Spice Rack', *National Geographic: The Plate*, 16 May 2014, at www.theplate.nationalgeographic.com.

15 Smith, *Peppers: The Domesticated Capsicums*, p. 8.

16 DeWitt, *Precious Cargo*, p. 238.

17 Lizzie Collingham, *Curry: A Tale of Cooks and Conquerors* (London, 2006), p. 51.

18 K. T. Achaya, *Indian Food: A Historical Companion*

(New Delhi, 1994), p. 227.

19 Navroji Framji, *Indian Cookery 'Local' for Young Housekeepers* (Bombay, 1887), p. 70.

20 Leela Punyaratabandhu, 'Massaman (Matsaman) Curry Recipe', *She Simmers Thai Cooking,* http://shesimmers.com, accessed 14 January 2015.

21 King Chulalongkorn, *Klai Ban (Far from Home)* (Bangkok, 1965), vol. I, p. 626.

22 David Thompson, *Thai Food* (New York, 2002), p. 145.

23 Andrea Nguyen, 'The Original Sriracha', *Bon Appetit*, www.bonappetit.com, 4 March 2013.

24 DeWitt, *Precious Cargo*, p. 335.

25 Melissa Block, 'Savoring the Spice in Kung Pao Chicken', *National Public Radio*, www.npr.org, 6 August 2008.

26 Ibid.

27 Naomichi Ishige, *History and Culture of Japanese Food* (Abingdon, 2011), pp. 84 and 96.

28 Ibid.

29 Richard G. Olmstead et al., 'Phylogeny and Provisional Classification of the Solanaceae Based on Chloroplast DNA', in *Solanaceae* IV (2009), pp. 111–37.

30 Michael Pettid, *Korean Cuisine: An Illustrated History* (London, 2008), p. 45.

31 Y. H. Hui et al., *Handbook of Vegetable Preservation and Processing* (New York, 2003), pp. 190–91.

32 William Shurtleff and Akiko Aoyagi, *History of Soybeans and Soyfoods in Korea, and in Korean Cookbooks, Restaurants, and Korean Work with Soyfoods Outside Korea* (Lafayette, LA, 2014), p. 619.

33 'Robin Cook's Chicken Tikka Masala Speech', *The Guardian*, www.theguardian.com, accessed 23 January 2015.

4 Healing Properties

1 Michael J. Winkelman, 'Therapeutic Applications of Ayahuasca and Other Sacred Medicines', *The Therapeutic Use*

   of Ayahuasca (Heidelberg, 2014), p. 8.

2 Elizabeth Moran, *The Sacred as Everyday: Food and Ritual in Aztec Art* (Ann Arbor, MI, 2007), p. 58.

3 Theophilus Redwood, *A Supplement to the Pharmacopoeia* (London, 1857), p. 414.

4 John Collins, Esq., 'Two XXVII. Two Letters' from John Collins, Esq. of the Island of St. Vincent, addressed Benjamin Vaughan, of London, on the subject of a species of Angina Maligna, and the Use of Capsicum in that and several other diseases. Communicated by Dr. Adair Crawford. Read Jan. 19, 1790', *Medical Communications* (London, 1790), vol. II, pp. 374–6.

5 William Lewis and John Rotherham, *The Edinburgh New Dispensatory* (Edinburgh, 1801), p. 218.

6 Andrew Duncan, *The Edinburgh New Dispensatory* (Edinburgh, 1813), p. 71.

7 Ibid.

8 Ibid.

9 Samuel Thomson, *The New Guide to Health* (Boston, MA, 1822), pp. 37–8.

10 Ibid.

11 Ibid.

12 Alvin Wood Chase, *Dr Chase's Recipes; or, Information for Everyone* (Ann Arbor, MI, 1866), p. 141.

13 Mark Twain, *Autobiography of Mark Twain*, vol. I: *The Complete and Authoritative Edition* (Berkeley, CA, 2010), p. 252.

14 Zoltán Halász, *Hungarian Paprika Through the Ages* (Budapest, 1963), p. 145.

15 Ibid., p. 146.

16 Istvan Nagy et al., 'Pharmacology of the Capsaicin Receptor, Transient Receptor Potential Vanilloid Type-1 Ion Channel', *Capsaicin as a Therapeutic Molecule* (Basel, 2014), p. 40.

17 Ernesto Fattorusso and Orazio Taglialatela-Scafati, *Modern Alkaloids: Structure, Isolation, Synthesis, and Biology* (Weinheim, Germany, 2008), pp. 91–2.

18 Diego Durán, *The History of the Indies of New Spain* (Norman, OK, 1994), pp. 194–5.

5 Chilli Pepper Madness

1 'El Viaje Misterioso de Nuestro Jomer' (The Mysterious Voyage of Homer), *The Simpsons*, Twentieth Century Fox Television, Los Angeles, CA, 5 January 1997.

2 Manuel Aguilar-Moreno, *Handbook to Life in the Aztec World* (Oxford, 2007), p. 347.

3 Mary-Jon Ludy and Richard D. Mattes, 'Comparison of Sensory, Physiological, Personality, and Cultural Attributes in Regular Spicy Food Users and Non-users', *Appetite*, LVIII/1 (February 2012), pp. 19–27.

4 Paul Rozin, 'Preadaptation and the Puzzles and Properties of Pleasure', in *Well Being: The Foundations of Hedonic Psychology* (New York, 1999), p. 19.

5 Debra Zellner, 'How Foods Get to be Liked: Some General Mechanisms and Some Special Cases', *Hedonics of Taste* (New York, 2014), p. 204.

6 Colleen Taylor Sen, *Curry: A Global History* (London, 2009), p. 39.

7 Alan Davidson, *The Oxford Companion to Food* (Oxford, 2014), p. 252.

8 Ethel Meyer, *1200 Traditional English Recipes* (Bremen, 2010), p. 111.

9 Emma Pike Ewing, *The Art of Cookery: A Manual for Homes and Schools* (Meadville, PA, 1896), p. 290.

10 Frances Emugene Owens, *Mrs Owens' New Cook Book and Complete Household Manual* (Chicago, IL, 1897), p. 195.

11 Horace (English notes by William Brownrigg Smith), *Horace: Satires, Epistles, and Ars Poetica* (London, 1878), p. 139.

12 'Devilled Kidneys', The Foods of England Project, available at www.foodsofengland.co.uk, accessed 29 January 2015.

13 Edgar Allan Poe, *The Works of Edgar Allan Poe* (London, 1899), vol. IV, p. 134.

14 Ibid.

15 Ibid.

16 Edwin Sidney Hartland, *Primitive Paternity: The Myth of Supernatural Birth in Relation to the History of the Family*

(London, 1910), vol. II, p. 241.

17 Alfred Stillé, *Therapeutics and Materia Medica* (Philadelphia, PA, 1860), vol. I, p. 398.

18 Roberts Bartholow, *A Practical Treatise on Materia Medica and Therapeutics* (New York, 1876), p. 468.

19 Sylvester Graham, *A Defence of the Graham System of Living; or, Remarks on Diet and Regimen Dedicated to the Rising Generation* (New York, 1835), pp. 22–3.

20 Sylvester Graham, *A Lecture to Young Men on Chastity, Intended Also for the Serious Consideration of Parents and Guardians* (Boston, MA, 1838), p. 47.

21 Graham, *Defence of the Graham System*, p. 181.

22 Philip Leon, *Bullies and Cowards: The West Point Hazing Scandal, 1898–1901* (Contributions in Military Studies) (Santa Barbara, CA, 1999), p. 70.

23 Amal Naj, *Peppers: A Story of Hot Pursuits* (New York, 1992), p. 9.

24 Revd A. F. Hewit, 'The Land of the Sun', *Catholic World*, LVI/333 (New York, 1892), p. 309.

25 David Kohn, 'Chile Cheesecake? Definitely', *CBS News*, 26 February 1998, www.cbsnews.com.

26 Nick Kontogeorgopolous, 'Tourism in Thailand: Patterns, Trends, and Limitations', *Pacific Tourism Review*, II (1998), pp. 225–38.

27 Kevin Lynch, 'Confirmed: Smokin Ed's Carolina Reaper Sets New Record for Hottest Chilli', Guinness World Records, 19 November 2013, at www.guinnessworldrecords.com.

28 Menu for La Hacienda Restaurant in Albuquerque, New Mexico, 1954, and menu for La Cocina Santa Fe in Santa Fe, New Mexico, 1950s, at www.lapl.org, accessed 2 February 2015.

29 Janine Gasco, 'The Social and Economic History of Cacao Cultivation in Colonial Soconusco, New Spain', *Chocolate: Food of the Gods*, ed. Alex Szogyi (Santa Barbara, CA, 1997), p. 157.

30 Gustavo Arellano, *Ask a Mexican* (New York, 2008), p. 145.

31 Tim Richardson, *Sweets: A History of Candy* (New York, 2008), p. 326.

Select Bibliography

Andrews, Jean, *Peppers: The Domesticated Capsicums* (Austin, TX, 1984)

Bingham, Ann and Jeremy Roberts, *South and Meso-American Mythology A to Z* (New York, 2010)

Bosland, Paul W., and Eric J. Votava, *Peppers: Vegetable and Spice Capsicums* (Oxford, 2000)

Briseño, Rolando, and Norma E. Cantú, *Moctezuma's Table* (College Station, TX, 2010)

Campbell, James D., *Mr Chilehead: Adventures in the Taste of Pain* (Toronto, 2003)

Crosby, Alfred W., *The Columbian Exchange: Biological and Cultural Consequences of 1492* (Westport, CT, 1972)

De, Amit Krishna, *Capsicum: The Genus Capsicum* (London, 2003)

DeWitt, David, *Precious Cargo: How Foods from the Americas Changed the World* (Berkeley, CA, 2014)

—, and Paul W. Bosland, *The Complete Chile Pepper Book: A Gardener's Guide to Choosing, Growing, Preserving, and Cooking* (New York, 2014)

Foster, Nelson, and Linda S. Cordell, *Chilies to Chocolate: Food the Americas Gave the World* (Tuscon, AZ, 1992)

Friese, Kurt Michael, Kraig Kraft and Gary Paul Nabhan, *Chasing Chiles: Hot Spots Along the Pepper Trail* (White River Junction, VT, 2011)

Halász, Zoltán, *Hungarian Paprika Through the Ages* (Budapest, 1968)

Hearn, Lafcadio, *La Cuisine Creole: A Collection of Culinary Recipes, from Leading Chefs and Noted Creole Housewives, Who Have Made New Orleans Famous for its Cuisine* (New Orleans, LA, 1885)

Kennedy, Diana, *Oaxaca Al Gusto: An Infinite Gastronomy* (Austin, TX, 2010)

Naj, Amal, *Peppers: A Story of Hot Pursuits* (New York, 1992)

Pilcher, Jeffrey M., *Planet Taco: A Global History of Mexican Food* (New York, 2012)

Pinedo, Encarnacion, ed. and trans. by Dan Strehl, *Encarnación's Kitchen: Mexican Recipes form Nineteenth-century California* (Berkeley, CA, 2003)

Russo, Vincent M., *Peppers: Botany, Production and Uses* (Oxford, 2012)

Simmons, Amelia, *American Cookery* (Hartford, CT, 1798)

Small, Ernest, *Top 100 Food Plants* (Ottawa, 2009)

Smith, Andrew, *Oxford Encyclopedia of Food and Drink in America* (New York, 2004)

Websites and Associations

Botanical Research and Seed Banks

American Society for Horticultural Science
www.ashs.org

Asian Vegetable Research & Development Center
www.avrdc.org

Banco de Germoplasma de Hortaliças (BGH)
www.bgh.ufv.br

The Centre for Genetic Resources, The Netherlands (CGN)
www.cgn.wageningen-ur.nl

The Chile Pepper Institute, New Mexico State University
www.chilepepperinstitute.org

New Mexico Chile Association
www.nmchileassociation.com

New Mexico Department of Agriculture
www.nmda.nmsu.edu

Society for Economic Botany
www.econbot.org

United States Department of Agriculture
www.usda.gov

USDA Foreign Agricultural Service
www.fas.usda.gov

Seeds and Plants

Australia and New Zealand

Eden Seeds
www.edenseeds.com.au

Firework Foods
www.fireworkfoods.com.au

South Africa

Chillihead
www.chillihead.co.za/burn

The Great Chilli Farm
www.chillifarm.com

United Kingdom

The Chilli Pepper Company
www.chileseeds.co.uk

Nickys Nursery Ltd
www.nickys-nursery.co.uk

Rogueland Seed Co.
www.seedfest.co.uk

UK Chile Farm
www.chilefarm.co.uk

World of Chillies
http://www.worldofchillies.com

United States

The Chile Pepper Institute
www.chilepepperinstitute.org/cart/seeds

Cross Country Nurseries
www.chileplants.com

Seed Savers Exchange
www.seedsavers.org/onlinestore/pepper

Chilliheads and Hot Sauce

The ChileMan
www.thechileman.org

Dave DeWitt's Burn Blog
www.dave-dewitt.com

Fiery Foods Show
www.fieryfoodsshow.com

International Chili Society
www.chilicookoff.com

Puckerbutt Pepper Company
http://puckerbuttpeppercompany.com

Scovie Awards
www.scovieawards.com

Acknowledgements

Thank you to Mara Collins, Art Edwards, Sarah Gilbert, Rebecca Kelley, Mark Russell and Michael Zeiss. My writing becomes less dreadful every day thanks to your shrewd feedback.

Thanks to Ken Albala, Andrew Smith, Dave DeWitt, Jeffrey Pilcher and the Association for the Study of Food and Society, for your knowledge on the spread of New World foods and for letting me spitball my own harebrained theories.

Thank you, Chris Onstad, Andrea Damewood and Steve Humphrey for being on board while I tasted my way through more chillies than is probably healthy. Thanks to Lents International Farmer's Market, Nick Zukin, Doug Kenck-Crispin and Los Roast for allowing me to lurk, take photos and ask questions.

Special thanks to my husband Scott Anderson for sacrificing precious refrigerator space to make room for a dozen bottles of hot sauce, and for the gastric fortitude required to taste it all. This book is lovingly dedicated to him.

Photo Acknowledgements

The author and publishers wish to express their thanks to the below sources of illustrative material and/or permission to reproduce it. Some locations of works are given below rather than in the captions.

Photos author: pp. 10, 14, 16, 20, 27, 36, 37, 40, 50, 51, 54, 58, 59, 68, 71, 73, 76, 77, 78, 88, 109; Bodleian Library, University of Oxford (MS Arch. Selden. A. 1, *Codex Mendoza*): p. 90; Rembert Dodoens, *Stirpium historiae pemptades* . . . (Antwerp, 1583): pp. 11, 24, 60, 65; Leonhart Fuchs, *De historia stirpium commentarii* . . ., illustrated by Albrecht Meyer, Heinrich Füllmaurer and Vitus Rudolph Speckle (Basel, 1542): pp. 12, 44; photo Amy Holsinger: p. 55; photos Library of Congress, Washington, DC (Prints and Photographs Division – US Farm Security Administration/Office of War Information): pp. 32 (Russell Lee), 33 (Russell Lee), 34 (Russell Lee), 38, 41 (Russell Lee); Massachusetts College of Pharmacy and Health Sciences, Henrietta Benedictis Health Sciences Library, College Yearbook (1910): p. 15; photos National Library of Medicine, Bethesda, Maryland: pp. 67 (from Elizabeth Blackwell, *A Curious Herbal* . . . [London, 1737–9]), 84 (engraving Oliver Pelton), 86; photo New York Public Library: p. 102; photo Randal Shepard: p. 26; photo Jack Specht, University of Texas at San Antonio (UTSA Special Collections – Institute of Texan Cultures, San Antonio Light Photograph Collection), reproduced courtesy of UTSA and San Antonio Express/ZUMAPRESS: p. 42;

conditions imposed by a Creative Commons Attribution-NoDerivs 2.0 Generic license.

Readers are free:

- too share – to copy, distribute and transmit the work(s)
- to remix – to adapt the work(s)

under the following conditions:

- you must attribute the work(s) in the manner specified by the author or licensor (but not in any way that suggests that they endorse you or your use of the work(s))
- 'no derivatives' – if you remix, transform, or build upon the material, you may not distribute the modified material

Index

italic numbers refer to illustrations; **bold** to recipes